D0936094

Margaret Deland

Twayne's United States Authors Series

David J. Nordloh, Editor

Indiana University, Bloomington

TUSAS 479

MARGARET DELAND
(1857–1945)
Photograph reproduced from
The Critic, February 1904

Margaret Deland

By Diana C. Reep

University of Akron

Twayne Publishers • Boston

Margaret Deland

Diana C. Reep

Copyright © 1985 by G. K. Hall & Company
All Rights Reserved
Published by Twayne Publishers
A Division of G. K. Hall & Co.
A publishing subsidiary of ITT
70 Lincoln Street
Boston, Massachusetts 02111

Book Production by Elizabeth Todesco
Book Design by Barbara Anderson

Printed on permanent/durable acid-free
paper and bound in the United States of
America.

Library of Congress Cataloging in
Publication Data

Reep, Diana C.
  Margaret Deland.

  (Twayne's United States authors series; TUSAS 479)
  Bibliography: p. 123
  Includes index.
  1. Deland, Margaret Wade Campbell, 1857–1945
—Criticism and interpretation.
I. Title. II. Series.
PS1533.R43 1985   813'.4   84–19154
ISBN 0–8057–7420–3

PS
1533
.R43
1985

HUGH STEPHENS LIBRARY
STEPHENS COLLEGE
COLUMBIA, MISSOURI

To Kay Whitford

187418

Contents

About the Author

Diana C. Reep is assistant professor of English at the University of Akron, where she is coordinator of the business writing program and also teaches courses in popular culture. She received her Ph.D. in English at the University of Wisconsin—Milwaukee. Formerly chairperson of the humanities division at Holy Redeemer College (Wisconsin), she is the author of *The Rescue and Romance: Popular Novels Before World War I* and coauthor of *Business and Technical Writing: An Annotated Bibliography of Books, 1880–1980,* as well as articles in popular and professional journals.

Preface

Margaret Deland was one of America's most popular fiction writers from the publication of her first novel, *John Ward, Preacher* (1888), to her last autobiography, *Golden Yesterdays* (1941). The peak of her popularity occurred during the sixteen years before America's entry into World War I. During that time she published her three most popular novels, four novelettes, and three collections of short stories. Although best known for her fiction, Deland also wrote numerous essays and poems, and two autobiographies.

Women writers in America before the publishing explosion in the 1890s generally wrote the domestic-sentimental novel or local-color story. At the end of the century Margaret Deland was in that group of new women writers who published serious fiction. Deland probed problems of ethics, human relations, and women's issues in her work. She was most famous as the creator of Old Chester, the fictional village where she set most of her stories. The generations of characters, the small-town atmosphere, the reality of daily life were all combined in Deland's fiction to produce a world that readers believed actually existed somewhere in Pennsylvania.

Throughout her career Margaret Deland was embroiled in controversy. Her first novel attacked traditional religious ideas of hell and damnation and brought vehement criticism by the clergy. She was later accused of advocating free love, approving of adultery, being a pacifist, and attacking women's rights—all because of her fiction. She exposed problems and conflicts with a fine detail and precise insight into the human psychology, and, as a result, those problems and conflicts often seemed serious enough to call for a radical solution even if Deland herself did not suggest one.

Margaret Deland was a moderate in her advocacy of change. She urged the dissemination of sexual information to women and worked with unwed mothers. She opposed divorce, saying it would destroy the family. Her writing is a mirror of the practical concerns and ethical issues that were part of the women's movement and society's transition from the nineteenth century to the twentieth.

Deland has never been the subject of either a biography or a full-length critical study. Until her death, she was frequently included in critical studies of the novel and the short story and cited as one of the nation's important writers. After her death, however, she was relegated to brief mention in literary histories, and her work faded from attention. The renewed critical interest in popular literature has resulted in greater scrutiny being given to women writers of Deland's era (Gene Stratton-Porter, Gertrude Atherton, Ellen Glasgow) for what their work can tell us about the times in which they wrote and the attitudes of their readers. A study of Deland has been needed as part of this examination of the influence of popular women writers.

There are few biographical sources for Margaret Deland. Deland's own autobiographies are excellent portraits of her world and her own thought, but they are restricted in coverage, one dealing with about three years of her childhood and the other with about thirty years of her marriage. Moreover, Deland did not write her books for the biographer who needed dates and names. Her autobiographies are introspective reminiscences of the world in which she lived and the people, famous and unknown, whom she met and knew. Contemporary interviews with Deland were genteel, reporters repeating her favorite stories but not apparently seeking significant information about her life or her writing techniques. Deland was a prolific letter writer, and her letters, scattered among dozens of libraries across the country, reflect her active life and her long involvement in Boston's social and literary circles. Reading hundreds of her letters gives a strong sense of her personality, her middle-class values, her devotion to her husband, and her serious attention to the business of writing. But there is little factual information about events in her life. She mentions surgical operations briefly without details, reflecting the gentility of her era when the well-bred did not discuss their personal problems even with good friends. Frustratingly, Deland often did not date her letters, and, even more frustratingly, she tended to avoid specific details, discussing acquaintances, friends, or events, for example, without naming them.

Since this study is the first full-length treatment of Margaret Deland and her work, I have included discussions of all of the fiction and dealt with the nonfiction as it relates to her major ideas. Chapter 1 relates the chronology of her life and the development of her career. I have relied on Deland's autobiographies, contemporary interviews, and her letters to construct the outline of her life primarily as it related to her published work and public activities. Her nine published novels are treated individually in chapters 2, 4, and 5. Because Deland's work is no longer generally known, I have included fairly complete summaries of the novels. Each novel represents a major presentation of Deland's thought on issues such as religious fanaticism, women's suffrage, divorce, and individual responsibility, and the reader needs the sense of the events of the novels to see, for example, the intensity of her opposition to fanaticism. The short stories and novelettes are discussed in chapter 3. Deland's short stories reflect particularly her great skill in creating a fictional world, each story filling in a piece of the history of lives and manners that made up the rural village of Old Chester and the bustling city of Mercer. Her other works, including poetry and essays, are covered in chapter 6. Particularly important in this chapter is the discussion of the two autobiographies she wrote at the close of her career. They show her great skill in evoking the spirit of a time and place and the revelation of a personality. Chapter 7 discusses the typical critical response to Deland over the years and examines her treatment of women's issues, her opposition to fanaticism, and her special talent in characterization.

Margaret Deland's work is especially valuable today for its picture of the changing concerns of women from the nineteenth century to the twentieth and for its depiction of the attitudes and mores of a society. Her treatment of women's issues presents both the need for change and the fear that too much change would destroy society. Because she was neither arch conservative nor radical reformer, her fiction more nearly reflects the intelligent middle-class American of her time. By presenting an analysis of her work and an examination of her themes, I hope to focus more critical attention both on her talent and her intellectual positions. Her work remains modern because the issues of which she wrote—fanaticism, women's independence, individual responsibility—are with us still. A realist who believed in the human capacity for good, Margaret Deland is a significant part of America's literary history.

Diana C. Reep

University of Akron

Acknowledgments

I am indebted to the University of Akron for a Faculty Summer Research Fellowship which enabled me to spend one summer in full-time research for this project. My gratitude goes to the libraries that provided me with copies of Margaret Deland's letters and writings: Pennsylvania State University Libraries, Western Kentucky University Library, University of Virginia Library, Barnard College Library, Colby College Library, The Newberry Library, University of Kentucky Libraries, Bowdoin College Library, Cornell University Libraries, Boston University Library, Allegheny College Library, Clark University Library, Massachusetts Historical Society, University of Vermont Library, Princeton University Library, Swarthmore College Library, Brigham Young University Library, State Historical Society of Wisconsin, Skidmore College Library, Piermont Morgan Library, University of Rochester Library, Washington State University Library, The Free Library of Philadelphia, University of Michigan Library, New Hampshire Historical Society, Wagner College Library, Wellesley College Library, Redwood Library and Athenaeum, Sweet Briar College Library, University of California at Berkeley Library, University of Oklahoma at Norman Library, Johns Hopkins University Library, Loyola University of Chicago Library, National Park Service at Morristown National Historical Park Library. Acknowledgment is made to Houghton Library, Harvard University, for permission to quote from Margaret Deland's letter to Edward Sandford Martin.

Special thanks must go to Sally Mitchell, Temple University, for her advice and encouragement. My deepest gratitude goes to Kathryn Whitford, professor emeritus of the University of Wisconsin—Milwaukee, for her generous reading of the manuscript and her insightful suggestions. Finally, my thanks to research assistants Karen Dudra and Kristen Figg for library work, and typists Lori Brisbin and Sonia Lauro who transcribed my scribblings.

Chronology

1857   Margaretta Wade Campbell born February 23 in Allegheny, Pa.; mother dies in childbirth, father shortly after; at two weeks sent to live with Aunt Lois Campbell and her husband Benjamin Campbell.

1870   Contracts rheumatic fever with resulting St. Vitus Dance and weak heart.

1876   Studies industrial design at Cooper Union in New York; appointed Assistant Instructor in Drawing and Design at The Girls' Normal School in New York.

1877   Cousin Nannie dies.

1880   Marries Lorin Fuller Deland of Boston.

1881   Begins friendship with Phillips Brooks.

1882   Begins taking unwed mothers into her home to rehabilitate them.

1885   "The Succory," first poem, published in *Harper's New Monthly Magazine.*

1886   *The Old Garden and Other Verses.*

1888   *John Ward, Preacher* (novel).

1889   *A Summer Day* (illustrated poem for holiday gift book); *Florida Days* (holiday travel book); first published short story in the *Atlantic Monthly;* first published essay in the *Book Buyer;* buys summer home in Kennebunkport, Maine.

1890   *Sidney* (novel); first trip to Europe; begins interest in psychical phenomena.

1892   *The Story of a Child* (novelette).

1893   *Mr. Tommy Dove and Other Stories;* serves as chair of the Library Committee for Massachusetts for the Women's Building at the World's Columbian Exposition in Chicago.

1894   *Philip and His Wife* (novel).

1896 Aunt Lois dies; does diagrams for husband's book on football.

1897 *Wisdom of Fools* (short stories); decides to develop the Old Chester setting.

1898 *Old Chester Tales.*

1899 Uncle Benjamin dies.

1900 "Studies of Great Women" in *Harper's Bazar.*

1901 "Individualism and Social Responsibility" in the *Independent.*

1903 *Dr. Lavendar's People* (short stories).

1904 *The Common Way* (collected essays).

1906 *The Awakening of Helena Richie* (novel).

1907 *An Encore* (novelette).

1908 *R. J.'s Mother and Some Other People* (short stories).

1910 *The Way to Peace* (novelette); "The Change in the Feminine Ideal" in the *Atlantic Monthly* enrages both sides of the suffrage issue.

1911 *The Iron Woman* (novel).

1912 *The Voice* (novelette); trip to Europe.

1914 *The Hands of Esau* (novelette).

1915 *Around Old Chester* (short stories).

1916 *The Rising Tide* (novel); starts American Authors' Fund for the Relief of Wounded Soldiers of the Allied Nations.

1917 Husband dies; goes to France for war relief work, representing Authors' Fund.

1918 Heightened interest in psychic belief; attempts to communicate with husband; "Beads," war essay, in *Harper's Monthly,* brings criticism.

1919 *Small Things* (war essays); *The Promises of Alice* (novelette).

1920 *An Old Chester Secret* (novelette).

1922 *The Vehement Flame* (novel); now convinced of spiritual survival after death.

1924   *New Friends in Old Chester* (three novelettes).

1926   *The Kays* (novel); elected to the National Institute of Arts and Letters; participates in symposium on psychic phenomena at Clark University.

1932   *Captain Archer's Daughter* (novel).

1935   *If This Be I, As I Suppose It Be* (autobiography).

1941   *Golden Yesterdays* (autobiography).

1945   Dies January 13 in Boston; buried at Forest Hills Cemetery with her husband.

Chapter One

Margaret Deland:
A Gentlewoman and Writer

Margaret Deland was born shortly before the Civil War began and died shortly before World War II ended. She was a woman of two centuries, and her eighty-eight years spanned the change in American life from rural to urban, from genteel to brash, from the horse and buggy to the airplane. Her intellectual curiosity and practicality kept her interested in and involved with the rapidly changing world of the twentieth century even as she retained the standards and manners of the nineteenth; thus she could admire the increasing independence of young women while at the same time shuddering at their frankness. Her work reflected the conflicts she saw between the old and the new.

Early Life

Margaretta Wade Campbell was born on February 23, 1857, in Allegheny, a suburb of Pittsburgh, Pennsylvania. She wrote in her autobiography *Golden Yesterdays*[1] that she was a descendant of the Englishwoman Elizabeth Gaunt, who was burned at the stake for high treason after helping one of the Duke of Monmouth's followers escape the bloody justice of Judge Jeffreys after Monmouth's execution in 1685. The spirit of the plucky Elizabeth showed up in the American Maggie who never missed an opportunity to express her independence and to ignore any resulting cries of outrage.

Maggie's mother died in childbirth, and her elderly father died shortly after. At the age of two weeks the baby went to live with her aunt and uncle, Lois and Benjamin Bakewell Campbell, at the family estate of Maple Grove, on the Ohio River near Allegheny. The Maple Grove estates were almost a separate village since the grandchildren of the original owner had all

built homes there, and there were dozens of cousins to play
together. Nearby was the village of Manchester, destined to
become the Old Chester in Margaret Deland's best works. Since,
coincidentally, her mother and her aunt had both married men
named Campbell, Maggie's name matched her cousins'. The
aunt and uncle became "Mama" and "Papa" as soon as she
could talk.

The family Margaret Campbell had joined lived the Southern
life of open hospitality, with assorted relatives, travelers, and
stray dogs. Yankee thrift was not an admired trait there; when
young Maggie tried to collect the going rate of ten cents per
one thousand weeds dug out of the yard, her aunt refused to
pay because the weeds were only seedlings and easy to dig.[2]
Children were not to think of profit and money. They were
to grow up untainted by mercenary impulses, interested only
in the refined things of life. Maggie's interest in profit, however,
never left her, and years later the writer Margaret Deland would
be known in publishing circles for having a sharp business sense
and driving a hard bargain.

In contrast to the relaxed Southern life-style, the religious
atmosphere at Maple Grove reflected the stern Presbyterianism
of New England. On Sunday the children were expected to
memorize four Bible verses and one hymn verse. In the evening
Mrs. Campbell read Bible stories to them. The sober influence
of the strict Presbyterian creed with its emphasis on hell and
damnation was blunted somewhat when the little girl spent an
occasional weekend with her maternal grandparents in Pittsburgh. The Wades were Episcopalian, and even though Maggie
still had to memorize her verses, religious activity took less of
the Sunday in their home than it did at Maple Grove. The
child probably paid little attention to the religious differences
in the two households. As an adult, however, Deland rejected
many of the orthodox tenets she had learned, and her first novel,
John Ward, Preacher, was a direct attack on the strict Presbyterianism of her childhood.

For the child, however, Sunday was merely an interruption
in her play. Maggie's childish games were made more exciting
in 1863 when southwestern Pennsylvania was in constant danger
of Rebel raids. The thrill of fear whenever Morgan's Raiders
were mentioned added to the daily excitement of playing "beating the Rebels." When not playing war, she occupied herself

with assorted pets, both willing and unwilling. Her childhood memories include making a hospital for bugs and then making coffins for those that did not survive her care. A pet chicken named "Anatomy of Melancholy," dogs, frogs, snakes were companions as she grew up surrounded by the love and protection of her family.

When she was thirteen, she contracted rheumatic fever, but there is no indication that she was seriously weakened by the attack. Her energy remained high. Her imagination was even higher. She told an interviewer in 1899 that her ambitions had been "divided between being a sculptor, an author, or a circus rider, and the latter was secretly the most alluring. But I feared it would not be approved and so I was resigned to the labor of authorship. . . . My first story was patiently and good-naturedly criticized by my mother as having an undue excess of adjectives. These salutary snubs cooled the ardor of authorship and then sculpture reigned."[3]

The family library was large, and young Margaret Campbell read the best it had to offer. Shakespeare, Hawthorne, Scott, and Defoe were on her reading list, along with the *Tatler* and the *Spectator*—all first approved by her aunt. Mrs. Campbell did not disapprove of Maggie's verses and stories, but she did not want her to submit them to magazines because early success might make the girl too proud and ambitious. Years later Deland agreed, saying, "If, at thirteen or fourteen, anything I had written had been printed, I should not only have become an insufferable youngster, but I should probably have let off whatever steam there was in me, and when I grew up, would never have written anything."[4]

When she was sixteen, Margaret Campbell got engaged to a neighbor who was thirty-eight and in debt to her uncle. Her aunt put a quick end to the notion of marriage. The idea of being engaged had been more exciting than the man involved, but Margaret was sent off to school at Pelham Priory, near New Rochelle, New York, to make sure she had other things to think about. Pelham Priory was an exclusive boarding school open to girls from good families. Though religion was stressed at the school, the girls also studied algebra, English literature, Latin, art, and German. Margaret was not very studious and was occasionally reprimanded for "indecorum" (*GY,* 27).

During the year she was away at school, the Maple Grove

estates were annexed by the city of Allegheny. All the Campbells
and their cousins then moved about thirty miles up the Allegheny River to the outskirts of a tiny village called Parnassus.
Although she went home that summer to the new family estate
called Fairfield, Margaret Campbell no longer felt she belonged
there. More and more she wanted to be independent and earn
her own living, although she knew that in 1874 nice girls didn't
consider such a thing. She also began to be conscious that she
was not really a daughter here. This feeling did not stem from
any change in the family's attitude toward her; rather, Margaret
Campbell had begun to feel trapped in the tranquil, rural area
with its narrow social life and strict religious standards.

The next winter was spent with a Quaker aunt and uncle in
Allegheny, who were not at all shocked at the idea of a young
woman earning her own living. Her attempt to open a school
failed, and Margaret Campbell had to face the fact that she
was not well equipped for her independence. At nineteen she
managed to enroll "with the patient and disapproving assistance
of my family" at Cooper Union in New York (GY, 50). There
she stayed with a friend from Pelham Priory and studied design,
perspective, freehand and geometrical drawing.

After this year her break with her family began in earnest.
She did not go home for the summer but instead went with
friends to Vermont. In the fall she got a job as Assistant Instructor in Drawing and Design at the Girls' Normal School (now
Hunter College of the City of New York). Her salary was eight
hundred dollars a year, and she was independent at last.

A vacation with other teachers in Vermont the following summer was important for several reasons. When, in August, 1877,
word came that her "sister" Nannie had died, Margaret was
in bed with a slight spine injury and could not go home. But
there was no possibility of going home; by taking that vacation
her estrangement from her family had now become serious.
"I had caused them pain," she wrote later; "Nannie had given
me all the generous heart of a sister—and I had preferred a
stranger, a school acquaintance, to her!" (GY, 59). Two years
passed before she was invited to "visit."

The second major event of the summer was her introduction
to unorthodox ideas about religion. The teachers from Boston
were Unitarians, and Margaret Campbell from Pennsylvania was
the sole defender of the theory of damnation. The Unitarian

teachers were polite and friendly, but for the first time she realized that the ideas she had grown up with were not shared by all. Never before had she had such conversations about politics, Darwin, the Dred Scott decision, and religion. All were new ideas to her, and for the first time she began to apply reason to questions of faith.

The third important event of that summer was meeting Miss Emily Deland, one of the Boston schoolteachers. They corresponded all the next winter. When summer, 1878, came and all the teachers gathered in Vermont for vacation, Emily's brother came to vacation there, too. Margaret Campbell's recollection sixty-three years later was that Lorin Fuller Deland arrived on the five o'clock stage, and that at 9:30 P.M. "They fell in Love" (*GY,* 68).

The two came from rather different backgrounds. Lorin Deland's family were Unitarians of modest income with that Yankee thrift that Margaret Campbell had always been warned against. Enthusiastically, however, the lovers made plans to budget and use old furniture from Mrs. Deland's attic. Lorin Deland had six hundred dollars in the bank and expected his father to raise his salary at Deland & Son's printing and publishing business when he married. The religious difference seemed no obstacle, since Margaret Campbell blithely assumed that she would convert the entire Deland family to Presbyterianism after the wedding.

The engagement softened some of the strained feelings with her family. Mrs. Campbell made inquiries and found that the Deland family was respectable. Letters started back and forth again. A few months before the wedding Lorin Deland's father died suddenly, but the plans went on. On May 12, 1880, at home at Fairfield, Margaret Campbell became Margaret Deland.

Boston and Controversy

After living a year with Lorin Deland's widowed mother, the newlyweds bought an old house and set up housekeeping on $125 a month. Various economy measures were instituted, such as raising chickens and making most of their furniture themselves. Community activities absorbed them. Lorin Deland became interested in local politics.

Both started to attend Trinity Episcopal Church, Boston,

where the great preacher Phillips Brooks held the Sunday congregations spellbound with his sermons. The couple became friends with Brooks, a friendship that Deland always felt was one of the most important in her life; until Brooks's death Deland looked to him for advice on her writing, her charities, and her spiritual doubts. In 1882 Lorin Deland gave up his Unitarian faith and was confirmed in Trinity Church, horrifying his family by accepting a faith that his wife herself was to leave only a few years later.

Margaret Deland lived an active life those first years in Boston. She wanted children, but none came. So she turned to helping unwed mothers, a charity project that remained one of her major interests all her life. For four years she took unwed mothers with their newborn babies into her home to try to give them a fresh start. She wrote in *Golden Yesterdays* that she became conscious of "fallen women" during a trip to New York where she saw women beckoning to men on the street. Deland and her husband decided that if unwed mothers could be helped to find work, their babies would be a "strengthening" influence in their lives. Knowing little about babies, Deland visited the New England Hospital for Women and Children and discovered that the Church of the Disciples in Boston had a committee to place these young women in homes. Soon she was rescuing a succession of forlorn young women. Over the next four years at least sixty young mothers with their babies came to live with the Delands, staying two weeks or longer until work was found for them, usually as domestic help to farmers' wives. Deland later said only six or seven young women failed to build respectable lives after they left her. Friends who expressed fears for Deland's personal morals in such an atmosphere were ignored. She was developing her own moral code and realizing that she cared little for either formal religious creeds or the rules of "respectable society."

When the Delands moved to a smaller house, the mothers and their babies no longer stayed with them, but Deland never lost her interest in the problem and continued to help where she could. In a 1907 article in the *Ladies' Home Journal* she said parents had a duty to give their daughters the facts of life. "It is for them to keep the mystery sacred in their children's minds by the defense of knowledge; by the honor and dignity and tenderness of truth!'"⁵ Over the years, she said, nearly one hundred young women had told her their wretched stories, and most blamed their problems on ignorance of sex. More than ten years after the *Ladies' Home Journal* article appeared, Deland wrote a pamphlet for the House of Mercy in Boston, telling the story of "Delia" and how young women in her predicament were helped by the shelter. Deland criticized the "respectable" people who did nothing but shunt aside such women in order to protect themselves from immorality. "There is a still deeper necessity, which is to do justly, and to love mercy."⁶

Several of Deland's short stories deal with the problem of the unwed mother. In "The Eliots' Katy" (1924), one of her best character portraits, she shows the rough, awkward Katy toiling as a servant to support her daughter Clarissa; the picture is an extremely sympathetic one. However, Deland also said that not all women could be rescued from sin; in "One Woman's Story—A Study" published in *Cosmopolitan* in 1896 (later reprinted as "The Law, or the Gospel") Nellie Sherman does not want to be saved.

While she worked with unwed mothers, Margaret Deland also kept house, painted china for extra money, and taught children natural history. She also began to compose verses, at first just fragments on brown wrapping paper, but finally full poems. Lucy Derby, a friend from Trinity Church, became excited about them and showed them to the Boston literary elite—Thomas Bailey Aldrich, Julia Ward Howe, Oliver Wendell Holmes. These greats liked Deland's work. Encouraged, Deland took some verses to Louis Prang, a manufacturer of Christmas cards, who began buying them to enhance his cards. Impatient with such small success for her friend, Lucy Derby also sent some of Deland's poems to Henry Mills Alden, editor of *Harper's New Monthly Magazine.* In the March, 1885, issue "The Succory" appeared. Other poems followed in *Harper's Monthly* and *The Century.*

In 1886 Deland published *The Old Garden and Other Verses,* dedicated to Lucy Derby. Deland was still uncertain of her own judgment and, in fact, throughout her long career, always sought advice on her writing. For this volume she asked Phillips Brooks which of her poems she ought to include. He told her to rely on her instincts. Her instincts evidently were right because the first one thousand copies of *The Old Garden* sold within a week. The book was bound in flowered fabric, making it an attractive gift item. The verses included sentimental descriptions of various flowers, poems on nature, love, and some verses for children. Although the repetition of set phrases and themes and the obvious imitation of other poets make the collection at best a good example of nineteenth-century sentimentality, the success of the volume launched Margaret Deland into the literary world. In 1899 Houghton, Mifflin issued its fifteenth "edition" of *The Old Garden,* indicating the long-lived popularity of this thin volume.

In a casual conversation with Lucy Derby after the publication of *The Old Garden* Deland had speculated on the problems that would result if a husband and wife held different religious beliefs and felt strongly about them. Out of that conversation came the theme for her first novel and the book that would turn her into a serious writer—*John Ward, Preacher* (1888), the story of a strict Presbyterian minister and the conflict in his love for his wife, Helen, an Episcopalian, who rejects his belief in damnation.

Deland took nearly a year and a half to write the book. While she worked on it, her own religious code began to emerge for the first time. She realized that she no longer believed in her early faith. She no longer accepted the Trinity, the divinity of Christ, or the Apostles' Creed, which promised the resurrection of the body. "To drag down one article of Faith," she wrote, "is like pulling a chain stitch out of a seam—the raveling thread may run across the whole fabric!" (*GY,* 201). She clung to the idea of life everlasting in some form, but at the age of thirty the beliefs she had always accepted were disappearing. She asked Phillips Brooks if she had any right to attend Communion anymore. He replied that God would not wish her to stay away. "I do believe that any, even the least, sense of Him, gives you the right to come to Him; at any rate, to come to where He is and try to find Him there" (*GY,* 204).

Her family's reaction to *John Ward, Preacher* was simple horror. Her uncle offered her two hundred dollars to throw the manuscript away. Part of the family's shock came from the idea of a young woman writing about hell—it was unladylike. Dr. William Campbell, Deland's uncle and retired president of Rutgers University, settled the matter. He read the manuscript and announced that of course she could publish it—he only wished there were more men like John Ward in the church. The old man had missed the point of the book, but the family gave up its resistance. Actually, Deland had decided in advance to publish it in spite of her family and had consulted Phillips Brooks, who told her to go ahead.

The novel sold well, partly because of the vicious attacks on it. Ministers preached against its "attack on Christianity"; the Boston YWCA refused to put a copy in its library; Professor Edward Gardiner of the Massachusetts Institute of Technology was forced to leave a dinner party after revealing that the Delands were friends. Publisher Henry O. Houghton just laughed, "Abuse will help the sales" (*GY*, 223).

With the success of the book the Delands could afford a summer estate in Kennebunkport, Maine. The cottage, its barn converted into a study, became Margaret Deland's favorite writing place, and for the rest of her life she spent part of every year there. Lorin Deland had begun an advertising business as well as becoming a Harvard football coach for a time, and money at last was no longer a pressing issue. Deland, however, never lost her concern for money and was always aggressive in negotiating publishing deals. She often suggested special Christmas editions of her stories to bring in extra sales.

Immediately after publishing *John Ward, Preacher* she began to receive requests for her work. "Mr. Tommy Dove" appeared in the January, 1889, issue of the *Atlantic Monthly*. It was her first published short story and the first work to be set in Old Chester, the town she was to make famous. She produced two gift books for the Christmas trade in 1889, one an illustrated poem, *A Summer Day*, put out by Louis Prang, and the other a travel book called *Florida Days*, based primarily on other books about Florida and its past. In the meantime she was working on her next novel, *Sidney* (1890). The book was not very successful, largely because the heroine was artificial, and her refusal to fall in love because some day her lover would die struck readers as ridiculous. *Sidney*, however, was important as a further working-out of Deland's new moral and religious beliefs. It also indicated that she intended to deal with serious issues and did not intend to join the women writers of light romance.

Margaret Deland now worked steadily at writing. She wrote numerous short advice articles, including a series of four in the *Independent* on the value and theory of novel writing. She was regarded as an established writer, although her 1894 novel, *Philip and His Wife,* which dealt with the problem of divorce, did not sell well either. Deland was against divorce for any but the most extreme reasons, but readers saw the novel as an argument for free love; in addition, it was marred by long discussions of individualism versus social responsibility. Deland received praise for her minor characters, but little for the novel as a whole.

More successful artistically and financially were the shorter pieces of the 1890s. *The Story of A Child* (1892), a novelette published first in the *Atlantic Monthly* and a sequel to "Mr. Tommy Dove," created an incredibly realistic vision of the fantasy world of a child. Deland was on the way to creating her own world of characters, places, and family histories in southwestern Pennsylvania. The *Critic* praised it saying, "Here is a book that gives most marvelous, perfect pictures of the child-world."[7] That ability to reflect accurately the mind of a child was to be one of Deland's trademarks.

A collection of stories, *Mr. Tommy Dove and Other Stories* (1893), followed. Only the title story was set in Old Chester, and another story in the city of Mercer, which would come to represent Pittsburgh. Sales were less than Deland had hoped.

A second collection, *The Wisdom of Fools* (1897), contained four realistic stories with unhappy endings. In three of them Deland concentrated on women's problems—education, financial security, and sexual morality. Reviews were negative. One critic wrote that "Mrs. Deland is tormented with philanthropy. . . . she attacks the problems that are known as modern. . . . Glimpses of suggestive surroundings and descriptions of limp scenery serve to heighten the bad taste of the whole book. No doubt there is a purpose behind, but there it lurks modestly, too decent to join in the company afforded it."[8]

At this point, Margaret Deland had written three novels, all with unhappy endings. The two short-story collections also consisted of stories with downbeat and, in some cases, tragic endings. In spite of literary friends who talked about the importance of realism, Deland began to think that perhaps the public did not want complete realism. She still strongly believed in the importance of realistic detail and characters, but perhaps happy endings were possible, too. She began to think seriously of developing the Old Chester setting and giving her realism the gentle cover of the past. *Old Chester Tales* appeared in 1898. Of the eight stories only two had less than completely happy endings. Critics loved the book; the public bought it. The *Outlook* said the volume was "likely to have a permanent place in our literature."⁹ The stories were written to introduce the town, its families, its problems, and Deland's most famous character, Dr. Edward Lavendar, Old Chester's Episcopalian minister; he appears in all the stories, dispensing Christian rationality, wisdom, and sympathy.

With this book Deland dropped her association with Houghton, Mifflin and moved to Harper & Brothers. She always said she got along well with all her publishers, but she was also known as a hard bargainer, and Harper's probably agreed to better terms than Houghton, Mifflin did. Deland drove editors crazy by constantly rewriting, demanding to see new page proofs, and then rewriting those. She devoted mornings to work, writing in the library when she was in Boston and in the hayloft when she was in Kennebunkport.

It was well that she had a strict schedule for writing because her life was busy with other things. She was becoming popular on the lecture circuit, and in 1893 she also headed the Library Committee for Massachusetts; the committee contributed a book exhibit to the Women's Building at the World's Columbian Exposition in Chicago consisting of one hundred books by Massachusetts women and a catalog listing two thousand others.

Deland also had become a social leader. The house on Beacon Hill boasted a fig tree in the dining room where dinner parties were often held for the important people of Boston. As hostess Margaret Deland entertained Boston's literary lights: Horace Scudder, editor of the *Atlantic Monthly;* Henry O. Houghton; Julia Ward Howe and her daughter, Maude Elliott; Dr. Edward Everett Hale. Lorin Deland's advertising business was successful, and his business friends were also frequent guests. The Delands were in the center of Boston's social circles, active in the church, in politics, in charity work. Margaret Deland's love of flowers was widely known, and in the middle of the decade she began what became an annual jonquil sale to raise money for charity. A contemporary article noted that she was one of the first host-esses to use the chafing dish in Boston.

The only unhappiness in the decade came from the deaths of her foster parents and her beloved Phillips Brooks. Brooks died suddenly in 1893, plunging the city of Boston into grief. Deland's foster mother died in 1896, and her foster father died in 1899.

Margaret Deland's interest in the question of survival after death had been increasing during this period. She had returned from Europe in 1890 fascinated with the English Society of Psychial Research. She joined the Boston Society and began to read widely in studies of spiritual phenomena and case histo-ries of those who visited mediums. Her own faith had settled into a casual Unitarianism, the same faith she had once thought so shocking. The existence of love side by side with death in the world, however, was confusing. The search for proof of some sort of afterlife became one of her lifelong passions.

The New Century and the Greatest Success

In 1903 Deland published *Dr. Lavendar's People.* Once again the critics and the public loved Old Chester and its citizens. The collection included one of her finest stories, "At The Stuffed Animal House," dealing with euthanasia. The other stories also dealt with moral issues of responsibility, and the wise, old Dr. Lavendar settled questions with compassion and reason. Deland was compared to both Jane Austen and George Eliot, although the Austen comparison was most frequent. *Harper's Weekly* said the book revealed "a richness and maturity of power, a fertility of imagination, a deep and moving sense of the human drama."[10] Margaret Deland had found the right combination of charm and character to attract readers to the deeper issues she wanted to explore. Dr. Lavendar, her most popular character, was a composite of Phillips Brooks, her uncle Dr. William Campbell, and Lorin Deland. She frequently received letters from fans praising Dr. Lavendar and asking for the exact location of Old Chester so they could visit the town that seemed so pleasant.

The twentieth century was bringing Margaret Deland and others to an increased interest in the "woman question." Although the Seneca Falls women's rights convention had been held in 1848, the big push for women's rights, including the right to vote, began in the 1890s. The Women's Building at the 1893 Chicago Exposition, with its exhibits of art, music, literature, and crafts, was one example of the American woman demanding equality in politics, in the marketplace, in education, and in the home. Women were questioning their traditional roles. By the turn of the century the controversy over women's rights and women's place was in the pages of every women's magazine in the country. Anything about independent women was considered a good subject for an article.

As part of the attention being paid to women's independence, *Harper's Bazar* asked Deland to do a series of eight sketches called "Studies of Great Women." Her subjects included Cleopatra, Elizabeth I, and Charlotte Corday. The series was uneven, and Deland's reasons for choosing specific women are not always clear. More important, however, in this series she introduced her ideas of women's suffrage—ideas that received criticism from both the suffragists and the antisuffragists. Deland believed that since many men were not qualified to vote on the basis of intelligence, obviously many women weren't qualified either; to give all women the vote would only make worse the mistake made by giving it to all men. It was not a position calculated to flatter either side. Deland feared that the frenzy for equality and individualism would destroy social responsibility and the family. *Philip and His Wife* had displayed her views about the common good being more important than individual desires. Otherwise, she warned in a 1901 article, the world would see "a return to barbarism, a return to the beasts."[11]

Margaret Deland herself had a happy and secure marriage and sought her husband's advice in all matters. She did not deny, however, that changes in women's roles were needed. Her work with unwed mothers had introduced her to problems that nice women did not usually know about. She welcomed the disappearance of the empty-headed, helpless young woman of the past. She approved of the new woman who was physically active and intellectually independent. In a long essay in the *Atlantic Monthly* in 1910 Deland defended the change in women. "We believe in the New Woman, and we are proud of her."[12] Women, young and old, had become discontented with traditional roles and were demanding new opportunities. Deland supported more economic opportunity and more sex education. The danger in more independence for women, she felt, was that social responsibility might be abandoned every time it conflicted with individual desires. One result could be the rise of divorce and the collapse of the family. Deland acknowledged that divorce itself might be needed, but she flatly opposed remarriage, which she regarded as another chance for error. In the same essay she attacked what seemed like separation between the sexes because of the women's movement. Deland had contributed to the Women's building in Chicago in 1893, but now she criticized it because it separated women's creations from men's. "How much better if the few great things . . . had been placed among their peers, and not put aside as noticeable because women did them. Such insistence upon sex in work is an insult to the work, and to the sex, too."[13]

When Margaret Deland spoke of suffrage during those years, she took a moderate position between the suffragists and the antisuffragists. In the *Ladies' Home Journal* she repeated her opposition to universal suffrage. She said the antisuffragists were wrong in their claim that women couldn't take the time to vote, and the suffragists were wrong in their claim that all women were qualified to vote. However, she specifically attacked the idea that women did not need representation and could influence men through coaxing and pleading; she called that idea "particularly offensive to intelligent women."[14] And she also pointed out that the prostitute in particular needed the chance to express her opinions. At the same time she rejected the suffragists' claim that women would "purify" the political system. The only qualification for voting, Deland insisted, was intelligence. She wanted a qualifying test on issues and procedures for all potential voters.

Deland's ideas on voting were perhaps not very practical, and she was much criticized for her opinions, but she did not pull back from discussing the issue in various forums. She applied tough standards to women. In 1916 she labeled as parasites those women who let men work to support them and felt no obligation to serve in the community. Women, she said, were in the work force to stay, and she predicted they would march "shoulder to shoulder" with men "in the home, in business, and in the world of ideals!"[15] Margaret Deland's own happy marriage no doubt contributed to her moderate stand. She and Lorin Deland had always shared their work, their goals, and their ideas.

Her opinions about women's roles and responsibilities also were presented forcefully in her fiction during these years before World War I. *The Awakening of Helena Richie* (1906), was Margaret Deland's first novel in twelve years. Set in Old Chester, it tells the story of a fallen woman who discovers that she has to face the consequences of her actions and accept her social responsibilities. Dr. Lavendar and all the Old Chester cast are there, but the book also has a depth and strength that the short stories lacked. The novel had been difficult to write. Lorin Deland had had to push her and help her with the plot; finally, she had been hypnotized by a psychologist recommended by William James. It took another year after hypnosis to finish the book, but the result displayed her greatest talents in developing the character of Helena Richie and the people of Old Chester. *The Awakening of Helena Richie* was a runaway best seller. It was on the *Bookman's* list of the top six books nationally for three months and continued on regional best-seller lists much longer. It was the only one of the six top sellers that autumn to receive the unanimous approval of the reviewers of *Literary Digest.* Critics praised it, *Harper's Weekly* calling it "a masterpiece of fiction."[16]

Two years after this success Deland published another collection of stories, *R. J.'s Mother and Some Other People* (1908). None of the stories is set in Old Chester, and they deal with such disturbing issues as miscegenation and business morality. The collection received only lukewarm reviews. Margaret Deland was, however, already at work on the sequel to *Helena Richie. The Iron Woman* (1911) appeared to almost hysterically favorable critical reaction. The novel continues Helena Richie's story into the adulthood of her adopted son. Set in Mercer this time, it follows Helena, her son David, and his friends as they become adults and begin to repeat the mistakes of their elders. The most compelling figure in the book, the character that drew such wild praise, was Sarah Maitland, the woman who runs the ironworks. The *Dial*'s comment was typical: "a triumph of characterization, and assures for its creator a place among the masters."[17] *The Iron Woman* stayed on the *Bookman's* top

six list for six months and continued to head regional lists well
into 1912. By 1913 it had sold over one hundred thousand
copies.

Deland was in her most prolific period during these years.
In addition to the two best-selling novels she also wrote four
novelettes—*An Encore* (1907), *The Way To Peace* (1910), *The
Voice* (1912), and *The Hands of Esau* (1914). *An Encore* and
The Voice were reprinted in *Around Old Chester* (1915), her next
collection of stories, eagerly awaited by readers who now apparently could not get enough of Old Chester and its citizens.

A year later Margaret Deland published a novel dealing specifically with the issue of the "new woman": *The Rising Tide* (1916)
was an attack on extremists on both sides of the woman question.
The portrait of Fred, the feminist heroine who learns that some
things cannot be changed by law, was both sympathetic and
critical. As a study of feminism and the problems of changing
roles for women, *The Rising Tide* was praised for applying wit
and intelligence to the issues. In fact, the book is one of the
sharpest examples of Deland's ability to peel away pretensions
and examine human character.

While the woman question remained a topic of discussion,
another and more serious problem was developing. Deland had
heard warnings about war in Europe when she visited Rudyard
Kipling in 1912, but, like others, she dismissed the idea; it
was too unthinkable. By 1914, however, no one could dismiss
the warnings. The world was in chaos.

Early in 1916 Margaret Deland started the Authors' Fund
for the Relief of Wounded Soldiers of the Allied Nations. She
asked publishers for lists of writers and wrote letters asking
for a donation of one dollar. Joining her in this effort were
some of the most important writers of American literature, William Dean Howells, Winston Churchill, Hamlin Garland, Booth
Tarkington, and Kate Wiggin among them. Deland, however,
was the primary force behind the effort, the organizer and the
director. More than twelve thousand letters to writers were
sent out, and, by July, 1916, the fund had collected over two
thousand dollars. The money went to several organizations already working to assist the Allies. Edith Wharton was given
five hundred dollars for her work in French hospitals, and a
special fund for the blind soldiers of France, Belgium, and Eng-

land was given five hundred dollars. As more money came in, it was sent to other funds. Some writers on Deland's lists, however, were pro-German, and she found herself the target of their outrage; she was called ridiculous and narrow-minded.

On May 2, 1917, Lorin Deland died. Her husband had been a beloved companion, a constant encouragement when she needed help in writing. Their life together had been active and happy, each enthusiastically supporting the other, and his death was a severe blow. Characteristically, however, Margaret Deland set off into new activities rather than retreating into grief.

The Later Years

In December, 1917, Margaret Deland went to France to do war relief work. She took two young women with her as representatives of the Author's Fund, the young women to work at a YMCA canteen and Deland to write a series of articles detailing the suffering and bravery of the French citizens and the American soldiers, later collected in *Small Things* (1919). Deland's articles loosely followed her own travels in France, relating anecdotes about soldiers and civilians. Most were very clear propaganda pieces for the Allies. She apparently believed every atrocity story told about the Germans, and she repeated many of them in her articles, telling readers that "America must save the world!"[18] The one article that stood out among the heavily slanted propaganda pieces was "Beads," also published in *Harper's Monthly*. In it Deland concentrated on creating the atmosphere and mood of Paris in 1918, warning that hate could destroy civilization when victory came. Perhaps, she indicated, it would be best if the Germans won because then civilization would sink to its lowest depths and begin to rise again. "Beads" brought her criticism for being a pacifist and even pro-German, but it was also called one of her best essays.

While she was in Europe, Deland became seriously involved in spiritual phenomena. She now had a personal interest in trying to receive messages from beyond the grave: she wanted to communicate with Lorin Deland. In the early months of 1918 in Paris Deland held ouija board sessions and recorded a series of spellings that appeared to be messages from her husband.

Friends in the United States also sent her messages they had received via ouija boards. Such attempts to cross the silent barrier of death were popular in those years, at least partly because of the great losses brought by the war. Margaret Deland, like others, was looking for reassurance that she would find again the one she had lost. Once back in the United States, she held meetings for the Boston Society of Psychial Research in her home where the evidence of survival was debated. She read widely all the reports of spiritual phenomena and came to be regarded as an expert on the subject. In four articles in *Woman's Home Companion* in 1919 Deland explained the historical development of the English Society and discussed reports of psychic experiences. She insisted, as she always had, that rational evidence was needed to support the idea of survival after death. In spite of the lack of such evidence, however, she wrote, "from an entire disbelief in the possibility of the continuance of identity after death, I have come to feel that it is a thinkable hypothesis."[19] In 1922 she wrote to a friend that even though she would always seek rational evidence, she now was persuaded that there was survival; this belief came with "the assistance of my husband himself."[20]

When Clark University held a two-week symposium on spiritual survival in 1926, Margaret Deland was a guest speaker in a session entitled "Convinced of the Multiplicity of Psychial Phenomena." Her talk, "A Peak in Darien," discussed her religious conflicts. In her thirties, she said, she had been convinced there was no survival after death. She still rejected most "proofs" as coincidence or telepathy. And yet, she said, it is reasonable that "the Universe . . . that the Conscious Whole is made up of our consciousnesses."[21]

The fact that Deland now felt convinced of survival after death undoubtedly was related to her husband's death and her own advancing years. However, she had not easily changed her views. Her correspondence indicates extensive reading and questioning, and she rejected popular mediums of the day and their obvious manipulations. Her final definition of God and survival came after years of applying her rational mind to both religious dogma and scientific studies. Later, in her autobiography, she defined her belief: "Recognizing a Conscious and Infinite Universe, we know that in It we live, and move, and have our being. We are workers together with It. We are sharers in Its immortality! Oneness with Its will, is Peace, and we can endure. We call It God" (*GY,* 194).

During the years after Lorin Deland's death, while she searched for spiritual answers, she also continued to write. In 1919 she published *The Promises of Alice,* a novelette about a young woman struggling between her own wishes and a promise to her dead mother, and in 1920 *An Old Chester Secret,* a novelette that is one of her best studies of moral choice. *The Vehement Flame,* her first full-length novel after her husband's death, appeared in 1922. The story of the marriage of a thirty-nine-year-old woman and a nineteen-year-old youth, it offers a merciless picture of a woman's empty mind and inadequacy. Sales were good, but Deland got nasty letters because of the adultery in the novel. In an interview in the *Worcester Telegram & Gazette* (November 16, 1923) she commented on the protests, saying, "The only immoral books are those in which wickedness is made attractive."

Her last Old Chester collection was *New Friends in Old Chester* (1924), containing three novelettes focused on the struggles of women. Two of the stories concern women with children born out of wedlock; all three portray heroines who defy convention and display a will and determination stronger than the pressures that surround them. Deland had often solved a heroine's problems with marriage, but *The Vehement Flame* and these stories reject marriage as the solution to all difficulties.

Deland kept working steadily. She was sixty-nine when *The Kays* (1926) appeared. This novel, set in Old Chester during the Civil War, contains characters rivaling those in *The Iron Woman* for complexity and development. The story concerns a pacifist who refuses to fight for the Union. Deland vividly created the emotional imbalances of war psychology and the conflicts between reason and emotion. And once again she found herself under attack, one critic calling the book "moral and social propaganda" and a "pacifist tract disguised as fiction."[22] Deland had by now lost the war fervor of 1918, but she protested that *The Kays* was not a pacifist argument; rather, it was a study of love, forgiveness, and war.

In addition to her writing Deland remained active in society and on the lecture circuit. Her companion in these years was

Sylvia Annable, who had been Lorin Deland's nurse. The friendship and help of the younger woman gave Deland the encouragement to keep on writing. By 1928 she and Annable were
spending most of the year at Kennebunkport, Deland's favorite
spot, the home she had shared with her husband. (She had
built a memorial to him on the grounds—a stone bench where
passersby could rest while walking to town.) The winter months
they spent in apartments in the Riverbank Court Hotel in Cambridge and later at the Sheraton in Boston.

In spite of occasional illnesses Margaret Deland's energy
seemed limitless. She read constantly and dashed off letters of
praise to authors. She wrote to the Pulitzer Committee in 1931,
supporting a prize for Dorothy Canfield Fisher, whom she
greatly admired. She accepted lecture requests, usually reading
an Old Chester story and charming audiences with her wit. In
1926 she was elected to the National Institute of Arts and Letters, along with Mary Wilkins Freeman, Agnes Repplier, and
Edith Wharton. The only woman previously elected to the Institute had been Julia Ward Howe. Deland maintained her interest
in social problems. Although she had shown little concern for
the problems of blacks earlier, in 1933 she wrote *Confession,* a
fund-raising pamphlet for the Hampton Institute in Virginia.
The pamphlet contained her admission that she had been only
slightly aware of the problems of blacks until she was in Paris
in 1918 and a Frenchman had told her American democracy
did not protect the blacks. She praised the Hampton Institute
for its dedication to black education and appealed to readers
to be generous with funds even though the Depression was
gripping the nation.

Margaret Deland's last novel was *Captain Archer's Daughter*
(1932), set in Maine. The novel splits awkwardly into two stories; the first half shows Deland's powers of characterization,
but the second becomes only a weak, old-fashioned romance—
and readers wanted more than that.

At the age of seventy-eight Margaret Deland wrote her first
volume of autobiography and one of her best works: *If This
Be I, As I Suppose It Be* (1935) tells the story of her childhood
and her entry into reason and understanding. Written in the
third person, the book creates the world of a six-year-old. The
book is episodic, showing the little girl Maggie learning about

such things as honor, patriotism, love, fear, and truth. Maggie appears as a healthy little savage who must be civilized. "I admit," Deland wrote in the opening, "she is selfish, cold-hearted, joyfully cruel, with no love in her, and without a particle of humor" (*ITBI,* 7). This revelation of Maggie's mind over the gap of seventy years shows the origins of Deland's curiosity and enthusiasm for life. Maggie was an independent thinker; so too was the adult Margaret.

Deland had already started a second volume of autobiography in 1935, but age was slowing her down at last, even though she continued active correspondence with friends and spent most of the year at Kennebunkport. The second volume offered the story of her marriage, and Deland originally intended to delay publication until after her death, but Harper's talked her out of the idea, and *Golden Yesterdays* appeared in 1941. The book is a picture of married lovers who enjoyed life. It is also a tribute to the man she had loved and the years they had lived through together.

Margaret Deland died on January 13, 1945. In an obituary notice *Time* called her a "serene, soft-spoken gentlewoman, whose fictional probings into social problems shocked her generation."[23] From the beginning her insistence on reason had brought her into areas of controversy in her work. She had written early in her career, "For my part, I have no patience with that prudery which turns from a book because of its subject. It seems to me arrogance to despise any revelation of human nature!" Further, "all of the calms and passions of the soul belong to us!"[24] In her long career Margaret Deland had written about those calms and passions.

Chapter Two

The Early Novels

Religious themes have been important in popular American literature from the beginning. The New England Puritans and Pennsylvania Quakers controlled the early presses, publishing religious tracts, hymnals, and sermons. The captivity narratives, really the first American adventure stories, combined lurid descriptions of Indian massacres with pious praises of the merciful God who had saved the author of the narrative. Most domestic novelists of the nineteenth century relied heavily on religious tone and saintly characters to support complicated plots, all of which ended with Christian virtue rewarded and unregenerate evil punished. Three of the best-selling novels of mid-century were *St. Elmo* (1867) by Augusta Evans Wilson, *The Lamplighter* (1854) by Maria Cummins, and *The Wide, Wide World* (1850) by Susan Warner. The angelic heroines in these books helped convert and save other characters amid much discussion of faith, duty, and Christian principles.

In the latter part of the century, however, traditional religion came under attack by social reformers. A new emphasis on science and rational thought was developing. This interest in science was partly a result of recent inventions and partly the result of Charles Darwin's *The Origin of the Species* (1859). By the last quarter of the nineteenth century nearly all philosophical, religious, social, and scientific beliefs were touched in some way by Darwin's work. Popular novels began to stress vigorous action for social good instead of tearful reliance on the Almighty. The boom in industry, the conquest of the West, the rush of immigration, all these were creating changes in the traditional American view of the world. American labor was organizing. Social reform became a serious issue. Women became more active in demanding new opportunities. As people began to insist that they could change the world and its conditions, passive acceptance of God's will was no longer considered an appropriate response. However, with this shift in religious and social values, many began to fear that society would deteriorate. Articles railing against rising divorce rates appeared; serious concern about what independent women would mean to the family structure became general. The growing interest in what could be achieved in the present and in the individual's need for self-expression and fulfillment seemed to threaten the traditional family structure, which depended on an acceptance of duty and suppression of individual desires.

Margaret Deland was part of this atmosphere of change in religious beliefs. She was also one of those who worried about the family structure. Her first two novels demonstrated her rejection of religious orthodoxy, whereas her third novel rejected individual freedom when it threatened the stability of the family.

Religion and Feminism

John Ward, Preacher (1888) opens with the wedding of Helen Jeffrey of Ashurst and Presbyterian minister John Ward of nearby Lockhaven. Helen is the niece of an Episcopalian rector, Dr. Howe. Early in their courtship she shocks John with her comment, "Perhaps we all sin in original ways; but I don't believe in original sin."[1] She also does not believe in the literal interpretation of the Bible or the doctrine of eternal punishment.

John thinks he will save her soul, and proposes. Actually, both delude themselves into thinking each will change the other. Once married, Helen begins to shock John's parishioners with her obvious indifference to doctrine. She stops going to prayer meetings because she doesn't believe in hell, and the talk of damnation distresses her. The elders in John's church begin to pressure him to take his wife in hand.

This unusual marital situation contrasts strongly with the more conventional romantic dilemma of Helen's cousin, Lois Howe; she has two suitors and is not sure she wants either. One is Gifford Woodhouse, a childhood friend, now beginning a law practice in Lockhaven; the other is Dick Forsythe, a summer visitor in Ashurst whose mother encourages a match with Lois. Also in a romantic dilemma is Mr. Denner, an elderly lawyer who, having determined to marry, cannot decide to which of Gifford's aunts he should propose.

The action moves back and forth between Ashurst and Lockhaven, as though between the normal and the extreme. A crisis occurs when Tom Davis, an unregenerate drunk, dies in a fire while searching for a missing child. John, following his conscience, tells the widow that her husband died in sin and therefore is lost in hell; Helen, however, assures the widow that the man is not lost. Thus, she not only contradicts her husband in his faith but also in his authority as a minister.

In Ashurst Mr. Denner is seriously injured trying to stop a runaway carriage containing Mrs. Forsythe and Lois. Helen comes home at once to join her family and friends in the vigil over Mr. Denner. Although only shaken in the accident, Mrs. Forsythe insists she is dying and extracts from Lois a promise to marry Dick. As soon as Lois makes the promise, Mrs. Forsythe begins to recover. Mr. Denner, however, sinks gradually to death. Everyone's attention alternates between Mr. Denner and Helen's obvious conflict with her husband. Helen's friends and family care little about the theological aspects of the problem, but they are certain that a wife's duty is to obey her husband.

Mr. Denner dies. Dick Forsythe, no longer interested in Lois, goes to Europe without releasing her from her promise to his mother. When Helen starts the journey back to Lockhaven, she receives a letter from John at the stage office saying that she is banished from his home until she accepts the strict tenets of Presbyterianism. The situation now has become a conflict of wills. Dr. Howe thinks John is mad, but the solution, as he sees it, is for Helen to change her views: "It is the wife's place to yield; and while I acknowledge it is all folly, you must give in" (391). Helen refuses.

Dr. Howe travels to Lockhaven to talk to John, but John believes the separation is God's plan for bringing Helen to the true faith. His fanatical need to convert Helen takes precedence over everything. Months later, Gifford Woodhouse sends word that John is ill. Helen hurries to Lockhaven, and John dies that evening. After the funeral Helen returns to her uncle. "I have no faith at all," she says (459). Her life seems to develop a purpose when Lois and Gifford wed, and Helen is needed in Dr. Howe's household. Her usefulness to her uncle saves her from isolation and bitterness.

Deland's first novel was a strong attack on Calvinism and

fundamentalist religions. John Ward symbolizes the religion he believes in. Doctrine is everything, and he can make no concessions to human frailties, no adjustments for benevolence. The reality of eternal damnation lives with him daily. When Helen tells him that theological ideas aren't very important and wants to keep them out of her marriage, he is shocked because he believes that theological doctrine is the basis of daily life. His love for Helen is connected to his duty to save her, so he cannot separate his ideology from his marriage. He is stern, serious, and rigid, holding "with a pathetic and patient faith to the doctrines of the Presbyterian Church" (41). His rigidity of religion prevents him from comforting those weaker than he. When the drunkard Tom Davis is killed, John is sorry for the widow but "no human pity could dim his faith, and he had no words of comfort for the distracted woman who clung to him" (163). Deland presents him as a fanatic, a minister blind to human needs and unable to offer hope or forgiveness.

Helen is a complete contrast to John and symbolizes Deland's own increasingly liberal attitudes. Helen's hold on religion is "slight," and she has abandoned traditional doctrine for a personal code. "Love of good was really love of God, in her mind" (42). Shortly after their marriage she tells John, "I must believe what my own soul asserts, or I am untrue to myself. . . . And I do not believe in hell" (99). Helen's mind, in contrast to John's, is constantly questioning. "Why is sin, which is its own punishment, in the world at all?" she asks. "Why does He make love and death in the same world?" (303). These are questions John Ward has never asked, and, because he cannot even consider them, he cannot effectively comfort those who stray from the narrow path.

When Helen talks to the widow Davis, her concern is to soothe the woman. "I do not know what the preacher would say, but it is not true that Tom is lost; it is not true that God is cruel and wicked; it is not true that, while Tom's soul lives, he cannot grow good" (175).

Although Helen always tells her family John is loving and gentle, the picture Deland draws is of a man in the grip of a religion that has no tolerance for deviation from accepted doctrine. John has a duty both as a preacher and as a husband to convert Helen. This duty drives him to banish her as a way to make her accept his doctrine. "Therefore I say, before God, for your soul's sake, you shall not see my face until you have found the truth" (394). Helen has always believed these disagreements cannot affect her marriage. When she is faced with banishment, she alone remains understanding of John.

The other characters show the same contrasts in tolerance. Dr. Howe is realistic, dealing with problems on a practical level. However, Elder Dean, who finally forces John to abandon Helen, is without compassion. He calls Tom Davis's death "an awful example to unbelievers" (168) and tells John that Helen must be converted to protect the church. "Your church, sir, and the everlastin' happiness of her soul demand that this disease of unbelief should be rooted out" (232). The wife of another Presbyterian minister remarks to Helen, "If I didn't think the heathen would be lost, I wouldn't see the use of the plan of salvation! Why, they've got to be!" (252). The supporters of Calvinism in this novel are gleeful in their anticipation of hell for others.

Deland's attack on the rigidity of John's creed creates an extreme man and an extreme situation, perhaps somewhat exaggerated. It is difficult to imagine John and Helen marrying each other. A contemporary critic remarked, "Presbyterianism does not produce men like John Ward, and we doubt if it ever did in this century."[2] The vehement attacks on Deland by ministers and other segments of the public, however, indicate that the John Wards of America were perhaps not that far in the past. Many readers who were moving toward more liberal attitudes on social action may have hoped the book would help close the door on such religious leaders.

The most realistic characters in the novel are the minor figures. Mr. Denner is one of Deland's best portraits and there is gentle humor as he tries to decide which Woodhouse sister to propose marriage to: Miss Deborah is such a good cook and so practical, but Miss Ruth is so pleasant and artistic. He flips a coin but it goes in a crack. He tries to solicit advice, but no one will say anything helpful. He decides to propose to the one he sees first, but he sees them together. When he finally decides to ask the eldest (age before beauty), he is hurt stopping a runaway carriage and sinks into death.

His death scene strikes the right note of religious uncertainty.

Dr. Howe has come to tell Mr. Denner that he is dying. The injured man accepts the news but politely rejects Dr. Howe's attempt to read the prayers for the sick. He has the greatest respect for religion, he says, but would like to speak of it "as men of the world" (335). He asks Dr. Howe, "What do you suppose—what do you think—is beyond?" (336). Dr. Howe responds first with religious platitudes, but Mr. Denner waves him to silence. "Think how strange: in a few days—almost a few hours, I shall know all, or—nothing!" (336). Under Mr. Denner's calm gaze Dr. Howe admits he is not sure of what may be after death. "I—I don't know, Denner!" (337). He holds his friend's hand silently. In the conversation of the two men Deland shows the question that all must face and, in Dr. Howe's candid admission, the universal human uncertainty about what cannot be known. This scene, coming late in the novel, highlights the contrast between the religious viewpoints of John Ward and Dr. Howe. Warnings of damnation, such as John Ward would give, have no place here. In the face of the mystery of death the two friends can only sit quietly together and wait for one to reach certain knowledge of what is beyond.

The religious theme in *John Ward, Preacher* was the one that held the reviewers' attention and the one that caused ministers to attack Deland. Surprisingly, reviewers seemed oblivious to what was a very strong issue in the novel—the right of a woman to an independent mind. Helen's steady refusal to accept her husband's guidance in religious matters, even when threatened with losing her marriage and thereby her social status, and her refusal even to pretend to consider changing her views are the actions of an intellectually independent woman. In Ashurst society a woman could not have a truly independent life-style, and it is a happy solution when Lois marries and Helen can keep house for her uncle. However, Helen remains a woman with her own mind.

Deland always felt that women must use their brains. She had no patience with women who did nothing and thought nothing. Her first fictional heroine reflects her belief in the importance of a woman's intellect. Helen suffers from the conflict with her husband. When John banishes her, she is crushed at the thought of never seeing him again, but she never considers changing her ideas. "It is fixed," she tells her uncle. "It can

never be changed" (397). John has assumed that losing him
will teach Helen to accept his doctrines. He says that she must
suffer to find the truth. She does suffer, but her truth remains
her own.

Even though Dr. Howe thinks John Ward is a madman, he
urges Helen to give in. "See here, Helen, if the man is so
determined, you'll have to change your views" (390). Helen's
aunt, Mrs. Dale, agrees. "Helen must change her views. . . .
A woman should be in subjection to her own husband" (402).
Even the Woodhouse sisters, with no experience in love or
marriage, express the general social view of a wife's place. "A
woman ought to think just as her husband does" (193).

Helen's refusal to compromise her beliefs leads to a stalemate.
Deland did not support divorce, and so the only way to end
the conflict was with death. John's death symbolizes the dying
of the older, sterner interpretation of the Bible and of man's
relationship with God. Helen is the liberal thinker, reflecting
more modern views. It is the man who is chained unquestion-
ingly to the emotional, unintellectual position. The conflict goes
beyond religion; it is a conflict of authority. Helen rejects John's
authority. "I must be true, no matter where truth leads me,"
she says, meaning she must be true to her own ideas (391).

In the end Helen's resistance has altered the opinions of some
of the other characters. When Lois marries, Mrs. Dale says,
"If Lois will do as I tell her, and be guided by a wiser head
than her own, I have no doubt she will be very reasonably
happy." Mr. Dale asks whether a woman doesn't always expect
to be guided by her husband. "When he has sense enough,"
Mrs. Dale responds significantly (473). The belief that a woman
always must be subject to her husband has given way to an
evaluation of whether the husband is worthy of being obeyed—
a major shift.

By an odd coincidence, within a one-year period, three novels—Deland's *John Ward, Preacher* (1888), Mrs. Humphry
Ward's *Robert Elsmere* (1888), and Celia Woolley's *Love and
Theology* (1887)—all advocated rejecting Calvinism in favor of
a doctrine of love and mercy. All three were best-sellers and
centered on a marriage in which husband and wife held different
religious beliefs. Deland's is the only one of the three, however,
in which the woman takes the position of rejecting Calvinism.

In the others the wife clings to the old creed while the husband turns to a more liberal philosophy. Deland's independent heroine puts *John Ward, Preacher* in the small group of late nineteenth-century novels, particularly those by women, showing the woman who thinks for herself.

Love and Death

Margaret Deland's second novel was set in Mercer, a city she created to represent Pittsburgh. *Sidney* (1890) presents her personal interpretation of God and meaning in the universe. Unfortunately, Deland abandons her independent heroine here for one who has virtually no mind of her own for three-fourths of the novel.

The novel is the story of Major Mortimer Lee and his daughter, Sidney. Twenty-two years before Major Lee had been so heartbroken at the death of his wife that he vowed Sidney would never suffer that way. He teaches her that love and marriage must be avoided and that she must question rationally "whether it was probable that there was a beneficent and all-powerful Being in a world which held at the same time Love and Death."[3] Sidney grows up accepting everything her father teaches her. However, her unusual opinions are regarded as ridiculous by others in the novel, and, when Major Lee invites Robert Steele to his home to convalesce, a matchmaking neighbor, Mrs. Paul, is sure a union between Sidney and Robert will result. Sidney, however, does not like sick people, so her Aunt Sally cares for Robert, who is fighting a morphine addiction. Robert grows attached to Sally and proposes. Since Sally has not been affected by her brother's theories, she accepts. Robert's friend, Dr. Alan Crossan, meets and falls in love with Sidney but does not court her.

In another romance Mrs. Paul's son, John, is shyly courting Katherine Townsend, a poor music teacher who is raising her younger sisters and a brother. Meanwhile, Eliza Jennings, a young milliner, develops the fantasy that John loves her. Eliza's mother visits Mrs. Paul and accuses her son of breaking Eliza's heart. Mrs. Paul is furious at the woman and then furious at her son when she learns he is really courting Katherine. When she forbids John to marry Katherine, he suddenly defies her for the first time and says that he is taking a newspaper job in another city and intends to marry Katherine. Eliza, embarrassed that her mother visited Mrs. Paul and upset because she knows John does not love her, finds an old beau and brings him home to dinner. Before long Job Todd and Eliza are engaged. When Mrs. Paul finally meets Katherine, the old woman likes the younger woman's spirit, and she assumes she can keep Katherine under her control as she has her son. However, she discovers that, although the couple allow her to visit after they wed, neither they nor anyone else really cares for her, and she is truly alone.

Robert Steele begins to realize that he feels gratitude rather than love for Sally. After much hesitation, he tells her the truth and offers to marry her anyway. Sally releases him from the engagement at once. She becomes ill, and Robert, in guilt, returns to his morphine habit.

Dr. Alan Crossan engages in long, philosophical debates with Major Lee, both on the existence of God and on the necessity for love. Alan has a heart condition but believes "the joy of life—I—I—mean love, . . . while it lasts, is worth the pain of loss" (210). Because of his heart condition, Alan tells Sidney he will not ask her to love him.

Sidney abruptly changes all her views of religion, love, and death when she sits up with her dying Aunt Sally. By morning Sally is dead, and Sidney has found a new meaning in life. "No, not death,—" she tells her father; "there is no death. Life and death are one; the Eternal Purpose holds us all, always. Father—I have found God" (354). When Alan returns to Mercer from a vacation in the mountains, Sidney goes to him and they wed. Within six months Alan dies, and Sidney returns to live with her father. Major Lee is certain that Sidney will break down, but instead she moves deeper into religious faith.

Deland's second novel on theological issues failed to shock readers as *John Ward, Preacher* had and, instead, simply bored them with seemingly endless discussions about God and the universe. The major characters indulged in frequent debates over the question of how love and death could coexist in a universe under a divine plan. *Life* magazine commented, "It is dull, and filled with doings and sayings of uncomfortable people."[4] The religious discussions were tedious, and the main characters lacked realism. Sidney eventually comes to call God "that tireless, eternal activity which constitutes the universe; that energy which is in all and through all, pulsing in every atom, recognizing itself in the conscious instant of a man's life, creating and destroying, working towards its own infinite end" (363). Her insights are forerunners of Deland's later descriptions of her own belief.

As a heroine, Sidney is dull and colorless. She conducts long monologues on the problem of love and death and dutifully accepts her father's opinions. Then, in a reversal within one night, she changes all her beliefs. That a woman would decide to marry a man because she has come to a philosophical understanding of the universe does not strike a realistic note.

The novel comes alive, however, when focusing on the supporting characters. Eliza Jennings, the lower-class girl who falls in love with John Paul, is an excellent portrait of a girl who drifts into fantasy and then is crushed when reality intrudes. Her frantic efforts to regain her dignity by quickly getting engaged to an old boyfriend are appealing. She drags Job Todd to meet Katherine Townsend and tell her of the engagement so that she can publicly wipe away any hint of heartbreak. Eliza demonstrates the universal need for dignity.

Aunt Sally shows the inherent dignity that the weakest can call upon when faced with disappointment. Sally is a pleasant, kind woman, generally ignored by her family and told over and over by Mrs. Paul that she is stupid. However, the woman whom everyone regards as helpless and weak has her finest moment when she releases Robert Steele from his engagement: "Mr. Steele, pray do not be disturbed. Pray do not give it another thought" (286).

The most memorable character in the novel is Mrs. Paul, a cruel and vindictive woman, bitter because she had failed to capture the love of Major Lee twenty-five years before. In the end, when she learns that Sidney has married, she thinks happily, "How he must suffer! And to think that I was not at home to see it all" (417). Her years of badgering her son, of insulting and dominating Sally and others, have blotted out her ability to sense what others are feeling. When John Paul and Katherine, happy together, become indifferent to her, she is baffled. Finally, her servant Scarlett tells her, "We get our deservings in this

life, and you've got what you've earned, when you find that
nobody cares for you" (420). Mrs. Paul, in fact, loses the most
in the novel. In the end, she is the only character completely
alone and without love.

Divorce and Morality

Philip and His Wife (1894) was Margaret Deland's first full-
length novel set in Old Chester, the town her readers would
grow to love. Alicia Drayton cares for her invalid mother while
her father lives abroad for his "health." Old Chester residents
know that he uses that excuse to live apart from his second
wife, but a society that is horrified by talk of divorce or separation supports such excuses. Alicia's half sister from her father's
first marriage comes to summer in Old Chester with her husband
Philip Shore, their daughter Molly, and her friend Roger Carey,
an attorney.

The Shores' marriage is a failure. Philip, an artist when they
married and now financially dependent on his wife's money,
is struggling with his feeling that it is more moral to separate
than to stay together when husband and wife no longer care
for each other. Cecil, beautiful and intelligent, is not troubled
by the fact that she and her husband merely tolerate each other.
She has come to feel that love is probably "a temporary and
passing experience," and she is "much too philosophical to be
unhappy."[5]

Old Chester gossips currently are concerned about the question of whether a couple should ever separate. Prompting such
speculation is drunken Job Todd, who frequently beats his wife
Eliza, expecting her seventh child. Many practical people, including farm owner Susan Carr, believe Eliza and her children would
be better off without Job Todd. But Episcopalian minister Dr.
Lavendar insists that Eliza and Job cannot separate: "She took
him for better or worse. Well, she's got the worse. Let her
stick to her bargain and do her duty" (209). He is shocked
by Philip's idea that separation is best when there is no love
between husband and wife. "You are advocating free love,
Philip! Do you realize that? You are advocating free love!"
(211).

Another romantic dilemma involves Dr. Lavendar's brother,

Joseph, a music teacher in Mercer. He spends weekends in Old Chester and begins to think of proposing for the second time to Amanda Pendleton, a widow who rejected him years before. Joseph tries to confide in old friend Susan Carr, but she thinks his talk of marriage is aimed at her and becomes nervous and distant. Roger Carey extends his visit to Old Chester and becomes engaged to Alicia Drayton. In spite of his love for Alicia, Roger is strongly attracted to Cecil and often finds himself involved in long conversations with her.

Philip finally asks Cecil for a separation. "We pretend to be married, but we are separated; we both know it, but no one else knows it" (243). Cecil is amazed that he wishes to make a public separation; such things are not done in their class. She finally says she is willing to travel abroad as her father does. Philip tells her she is an unfit mother because she is self-centered and spoils Molly. They argue over the child, each wanting custody.

Cecil consults Roger about handling her money and settling custody of Molly. He is upset at the news of a separation, partly because he feels his attraction to Cecil. As he argues with her, Cecil becomes faint; Roger catches her in his arms and nearly kisses her. "Their eyes met in one full, pulsating look,—met with a clash of exultant shame; and dropped, cowering" (316). Roger leaves the house abruptly, knowing both he and Cecil are afraid of their feelings. He presses Alicia for an immediate wedding, but she refuses because of her mother. They quarrel and break the engagement. Cecil, in the meantime, tells Philip they cannot separate, but Philip refuses to give up the idea.

Roger convinces himself that he is imagining an attraction to Cecil and goes to see her again to help patch up her marriage. The two end in each other's arms, declaring their love. Again he tears himself away and this time decides never to return. He believes that no divorce could make his relationship with Cecil moral because divorce is immoral. He sends a note to her, telling her that he will never see her again. Stunned, Cecil decides to leave Philip and Molly and go to Europe. She no longer can maintain the pretense of her marriage, and she believes, as Philip does, that that would not be a good influence on Molly.

Meanwhile Eliza Todd's baby dies. Job Todd, in a drunken

rage, throws his eldest son down the stairs, injuring the boy's spine. This violence arouses even those who object to interfering between a husband and wife. Job is put in jail, and Eliza is free of him for a time. A new marriage in Old Chester occurs when Susan Carr changes her mind and accepts Joseph Lavendar's "proposal." As a gentleman, he cannot correct her mistake, and so they wed. At the same time Mr. Drayton returns home from Europe. His "friend" in Europe has died, and he no longer wants to stay abroad. Mrs. Drayton is upset because her placid existence is disrupted. Mr. Drayton's return, however, frees Alicia to leave her mother and marry Roger.

Philip and His Wife was the work Deland said later that she liked least among her writings. Yet the character development here is an advance over her two previous books. Cecil Shore is a fascinating and complex woman: she is spoiled and self-indulgent, but at the same time maintains a good house for her family, is pleasant to Philip even though she no longer loves him, and is generally good-natured and tolerant. "Even Old Chester had to admit that she was very agreeable to Philip" (27). In spite of her dislike of social forms, she understands the implications of divorce both to the family and to the society. Philip sees only his own narrow moral purpose and cannot visualize the possible future immorality stemming from divorce, nor the possible consequences to the children and the spouse.

Subject to moods, Cecil sometimes smothers Molly with love and at other times sends her away because the child's chatter is boring. Although she avoids Old Chester society, Cecil is capable of dealing with all social levels. She charms a drunken Job Todd into forgetting his intention of beating Eliza. She fascinates Roger Carey with her insightful mind and interesting conversation. She has accepted with equanimity the absence of physical love or companionship in her marriage. Philip is an ascetic in his tastes, close to a fanatic in his ideals. "He had thought to marry a beautiful soul, but had married instead a beautiful body" (82). After the first year of marriage, Philip felt he had lapsed into concentrating only on physical pleasure. He began to try to change Cecil—to change their relationship to one he could idealize. She, however, had no wish to change. "Oh, he ought to have been a monk," Cecil thinks occasionally (28). When Philip asks for a divorce, she thinks first there is another woman but then dismisses the idea: "You haven't blood enough in your veins for that. . . . you are not a man!" (242). In spite of her acceptance of a loveless but comfortable life, when she falls in love with Roger Carey all her sensuality comes alive. She loves him violently. When he rejects her, she hates him violently, but still realizes at once that she is becoming stronger and one day will forget him. Cecil has come to know herself better. Philip gains no insights. Like John Ward, he clutches an idea with a fanatical grip and cannot see any other possibilities.

Deland's novel was criticized as advocating divorce and freedom from unpleasant duty. In fact, Deland was firmly against divorce and accepted separation only to protect the children in such cases as that of Eliza and Job Todd. Roger Carey speaks for Deland when he says, "Mind you, I think separation is desirable occasionally but never divorce. . . . Divorce seems to me like suicide, not inherently or specifically wrong, but socially vicious; both lower just a little the moral tone of society" (229).

One of the reasons readers may have misunderstood Deland's position is that there is little in the Shores' marriage to save. Cecil is stronger, more intelligent, and more dynamic than her husband. They have no true relationship at all. Even more, *Philip and His Wife* contains other marriages that are disastrous. Eliza, who married Job Todd in haste in *Sidney,* repents her mistake in this novel. She is the battered wife, subject to the moods of a drunken husband, struggling to make ends meet, to keep her children fed and out of their father's way. The town tries to help. Dr. Lavendar "speaks" to Job. Alicia suggests that perhaps the community ought to take on the support of the family, and Susan Carr believes Eliza should leave Job. But good people are ineffective. Putting Job in jail frees Eliza temporarily, but a strong case certainly exists here for permanent separation. Later, in *The Iron Woman* (1911), Deland would show Eliza as a cheerful widow, free at last of her husband.

The marriage of Mr. and Mrs. Drayton is also a failure. William Drayton had married his second wife for convenience, to give Cecil a mother. After Alicia was born, Fanny Drayton had lapsed into a convenient invalidism, and William left for Europe. When he returns at the end of the novel, Fanny is visibly distressed. For years she has maintained the fiction that she misses her husband. Now he is home, and she is faced with an end to her comfortable life. They were both happier apart.

The three marriages in the novel represent little happiness, and, unfortunately, the future marriages seem no more likely to succeed. Roger and Alicia may not find happiness because he has suppressed his love for Cecil, and Alicia often seems childish and boring to him. The marriage of Joseph Lavendar and Susan Carr is the result of a misunderstanding. Since they are both good-natured people, they probably will be content, but the overall picture of marriage in this novel is bleak.

Philip and His Wife is notable for containing the first significant appearance of Deland's most famous character. Dr. James Lavendar (called Edward in later works), the Episcopalian minister in Old Chester, is the voice and moral conscience of the town. Moreover, he represents Deland's image of what a religious leader should be. Dr. Lavendar provides the rational advice and moral support his parishioners need to make the difficult decisions of life and to do their duty. In *Philip and His Wife* he firmly opposes separation for Eliza and Job. He warns Philip that ideas about divorce will destroy society. In later works the old man is less fixed by traditional responses and often demonstrates a practical, even unorthodox approach to the problems of Old Chester.

Philip and His Wife contains the most realistic characterizations in Deland's early novels. The marriages and the people who struggle with them offer readers characters and problems they can identify with. Furthermore, Old Chester in this novel begins to take on a personality that represents the nineteenth-century American small town, with its conservatism and resistance to change.

The three early novels, however, suffer from an overdose of moral awareness. Although Deland's minor characters show the promise of her future artistry, main characters often lapse into sermons. Deland concentrated on creating strong women and, as a result, her men were often one-dimensional. John Ward, Major Lee, and Philip Shore are all inflexible extremists, certain they are right, lacking human variety and complexity. The women represent reason and tolerance, but only Cecil Shore has the complexity of character to excite the reader's interest. All the early novels have unhappy endings, contrary to the expectations of readers of popular fiction.

At this point in her career Margaret Deland was struggling with the problem of presenting ideas without forcing characters to stand around and recite long speeches. Through her short stories she developed the ability to create believable characters who revealed ideas through actions. Twelve years passed before she wrote another full-length novel, but in the meantime she had created the world of Old Chester.

Chapter Three

Old Chester and Other Places

The latter half of the nineteenth century and the beginning of the twentieth saw a boom in magazine publishing in the United States. Highest in prestige when Margaret Deland began writing her stories were the *Atlantic Monthly, Harper's Monthly,* the *Century,* and the *Critic,* all read by those who considered themselves intellectual, conservative, and literary. However, more than just these groups were reading magazines, and various special-interest magazines sprang up to meet different needs. Further, the growing middle class and the developing technology in photoengraving and typesetting made publishing big business. *Ladies' Home Journal, McClure's Magazine, Cosmopolitan,* and *Munsey's* developed huge circulations while writers prospered. Not only were the magazines hungry for stories, but they paid very well; established writers might make ten thousand dollars for the serialization of a novel before publication. In such an environment it is not surprising that Margaret Deland published all her work after *John Ward, Preacher* first in the magazines.

Development of a Writer

Altogether, Margaret Deland published thirty-eight short stories, most of them in *Harper's Weekly* or the *Atlantic Monthly.* Nearly all were reprinted in the seven short-story collections published between 1893 and 1924. Some of the stories also were published separately as novelettes, often as holiday gift books. In addition, seven long stories were published first as novelettes, four of them never collected.

Most of her short fiction was set in the mid-nineteenth century. Deland preferred to write of the quiet world of the small town in the 1860s and 1870s, although a number of stories are set in larger cities. She wrote one mystery, "The Waiting Hand," for the *Century,* which had invited Deland, as it had Owen

Wister and S. Weir Mitchell, to write a mystery based on the superstition of thirteen at a dinner table. "The Waiting Hand" is actually more a gothic story than it is a mystery, including a severed hand and an unburied body in an atmosphere of decay and doom. At her best, however, Deland concentrated on ordinary people, caught up in realistic situations of human folly or pressing circumstances. Although she created the town of Old Chester in her first short story, "Mr. Tommy Dove" (1893), most of the stories before 1898 were set in other places. The two early collections, *Mr. Tommy Dove and Other Stories* (1893) and *The Wisdom of Fools* (1897), were uneven. Some stories strained for dramatic effect and failed. "The Face on the Wall," for example, is a bizarre tale of a drunken painter who destroys his best work and commits suicide.

The best stories of this period deal with women subject to financial disaster or struggling with moral crises. "A Fourth-Class Appointment" is, at first, charming in its picture of old Mrs. Gedge and her middle-aged daughter Amanda running a New England village post office. When the two receive notice that a new postmaster is being appointed, their desperation at losing their livelihood is sharp and bitter. "House of Rimmon" shows widow Lydia Eaton with her children, bravely leaving her brother's house because she cannot accept support from a man who makes money by exploiting his workers. Lydia struggles to support her family as a clerk; her decision is painful, but her conscience is clear. "Counting the Cost" considers the problem of a young woman educated beyond her social class, unable to leave the father she loves, but losing her lover when he meets her family. "The Law, or the Gospel," probably based on Deland's work with unwed mothers, is a strong statement about the uselessness of helping someone who doesn't wish to be helped. Socialite Sara Wharton squanders time and money in a fruitless attempt to convince Nellie Sherman to live a moral life. Nellie finds goodness dull, and Sara wonders if her work with Nellie has been worthwhile or only an expression of her own sentimentalism. The best of these stories explored the weaknesses and strengths of the kinds of people Deland knew from her childhood in rural Pennsylvania.

In all her early stories Deland tended toward a realism that reviewers, perhaps used to the romantic stories of other popular

women writers, called "morbid." Of the nine stories in the
first two collections, seven end unhappily. The two endings
that might be called happy come from marriages of convenience.
Always conscious of the reading and buying public, and disappointed with sales, Deland decided in 1897 to develop the world
of Old Chester. She also began to concentrate on endings in
which characters settle their problems and handle their responsibilities.

In Old Chester Deland created a physical setting so real that
readers wrote and asked her for its exact location so that they
could visit. The time she wrote about was the mid-nineteenth
century, when rural Pennsylvania villages were not pressed by
the outside world, and the daily lives of the villagers could
provide the themes of her stories. Most important, like William
Faulkner writing in Mississippi some forty years later, Deland
brought into existence several generations of parents, cousins,
and neighbors living in a particular region. The thoughts, feelings, and actions of the inhabitants of Old Chester and the larger
city, nearby Mercer, were cataloged in stories and novels for
the next thirty years. Faithful readers stepped into a familiar
world with familiar people as each Old Chester story appeared.
Characters played large or small parts as the stories wove the
history of a particular time and place. Mrs. Drayton, the invalid
mother of *Philip and His Wife,* is a formidable gossip in story
after story, commenting with grim satisfaction on the follies
of her neighbors. Miss Lydia Sampson, who refuses to marry
a stingy man in "The Grasshopper and the Ant," raises an unwanted child in "An Old Chester Secret." Lawyer Ezra Barkley,
who marries Maria Welwood in "Miss Maria," handles the legal
affairs of Old Chester residents in other stories.

The first two Old Chester collections were *Old Chester Tales*
(1898) and *Dr. Lavendar's People* (1903). Reviewers and readers
were charmed. Margaret Deland really demonstrated the
strengths of her talent with these stories, especially in "An Exceeding High Mountain," "At the Stuffed Animal House," "The
Promises of Dorothea," and "The Child's Mother." Later collections were *R. J.'s Mother and Some Other People* (1908), *Around
Old Chester* (1915), and *New Friends in Old Chester* (1924). In
R. J.'s Mother Deland left Old Chester and its problems and
touched on more controversial themes, such as miscegenation

in "A Black Drop." This collection, with no stories in Old Chester and only two set in Mercer, was less popular, showing that readers wanted Old Chester from Margaret Deland.

Initially, Deland used a strong authorial voice, interrupting the narrative in her stories and commenting on the actions of the characters, their mistakes, and the general implications of the conflicts. Her comments often pointed with amusement to characters' inconsistencies or with stern judgment to the social pressures that helped create the character's problems. In "Counting the Cost" the heroine faces a lonely life at the end of the story. Deland then directly discusses the situation with the reader: "What is the child's duty? To live her own life, or to live someone else's life?"[1]

With the publication of *Old Chester Tales* in 1898, Deland began to use a narrative voice that is never really identified but is obviously a woman who had grown up in Old Chester and who remembers the people of the village with humor and affection. Although Deland never fully developed the narrator into a character, a narrative voice that reflected personal knowledge of the events in Old Chester gave the comfortable flavor of gossip to her stories, making readers feel they were reading memories of a real time and place. In "The Apotheosis of the Reverend Mr. Spangler" the narrator recalls that, as students in Miss Baily's school, she and the other girls admired Miss Baily's brother, heartbroken over the death of a sweetheart. "We all knew that he was thinking of his bereavement."[2] Later in the story the narrator comments on modern education: "We were taught a certain respect for our own language . . . which our children do not seem to know. . . . However, this may all be sour grapes . . ." (8–9). Although Margaret Deland did not establish that narrative voice in every story or novel she wrote, she did continue to use authorial commentary extensively. Her remarks about characters' actions or the pressures of society defined the world as she saw it and offered readers her views about such things as women's roles, fanaticism, and duty.

The most fully developed continuing characters in the stories were Dr. Edward Lavendar and Dr. William King. These men, the first a healer of the soul, the second a healer of the flesh, provide the foundation for the Old Chester community. Dr. Lavendar is a composite of Phillips Brooks, Deland's uncle Dr.

William Campbell, and Lorin Deland. Those wishing to know
Margaret Deland's philosophy of human relations have only
to examine Dr. Lavendar. She took the name Lavendar from
the obituary column of the Boston *Transcript* and created in
Philip and His Wife a rather rigid Episcopalian minister who
insisted that Eliza Todd had to stay with her drunken husband.
In the short stories, however, Deland softened Dr. Lavendar,
making him firm enough to guide his parishioners into the right
moral choices, and wise enough to know that life often does
not allow strict interpretation of rules. In "The Child's Mother"
he refuses to give a little girl back to her natural mother who
abandoned her years before because the woman wants to pretend the child is a niece. However, in "Good for the Soul"
Dr. Lavendar advises a woman not to reveal her past sins to
her husband. In the first case, the woman has not yet accepted
responsibility for her actions and, therefore, is not a fit mother;
in the second, the woman wants to purge her soul by destroying
her husband's faith in her. In both cases, Dr. Lavendar rejects
the easy traditional positions of returning a child to her natural
mother and counseling confession of past sins. In these stories
the innocent must be protected.

The proper moral sense espoused by Dr. Lavendar is a combination of the rules of the church and his definition of individual
responsibility. He is keenly aware of the needs of his parishioners, and he knows that principles must sometimes be adjusted
to accommodate life. He destroys a loan agreement in "The
Note" so that the heir to an estate will not press a struggling
man for repayment. When retarded Annie Hutchinson in "At
the Stuffed Animal House" kills her cancer-stricken sister to
relieve the pain, Dr. Lavendar tells her it wasn't right, but then
makes her promise never to tell anyone what she did. In "Harvest of Fear" when he finds the Halsey daughters burning their
dead father's will so that their brother's widow and children
can share in the inheritance, Dr. Lavendar keeps silent. It is
the father's sin, he thinks, because the stern parent dominated
his children, trying to control them. Dr. Lavendar, then, protects
the living—the people who need help in the present. And he
tries to keep the way open for people to build better lives and
to be free of circumstances that crush the spirit.

In "Sally" Dr. Lavendar tries for ten years to find a way to help Sally escape the burden of her selfish family and marry her childhood sweetheart. In "The Promises of Dorothea" he encourages Oscar King to elope with Dorothea and free her from a dull, wasted life with her maiden aunts. Although he believes all women should be married, he is the first to understand when Lydia Sampson ("The Grasshopper and the Ant") spends all her money so that stingy William Rives will break their engagement.

Dr. Lavendar rises above all the Old Chester residents. He is the standard no one else can reach. The man who comes the closest is Dr. William King, who cares for the physical ills of Old Chester. He is the other person Old Chester turns to: solid, dependable, and practical. But although practical, he sometimes does not quite understand what moral decisions people should make, and his advice proves to be less correct than Dr. Lavendar's.

Dr. King advises Paul Walton in "The Third Volume" not to tell his brother Peter that he cheated in a game of backgammon when Peter's winning meant he would be free to commit suicide to be with his dead wife. Paul's cheating saved Peter's life. "Of course Paul must hold his tongue," Dr. King says to Dr. Lavendar.[3] But Dr. Lavendar warns him that a lie festers in the person who tells it. In the end Paul does confess to Peter in order to die with a clear conscience. In "The Voice" when Philippa Roberts confesses to Dr. King that she gave poison to Reverend Fenn, thinking it was a love potion, Dr. King tells her that she should forget about what she has done. But keeping silent keeps the guilt alive, and, when Dr. Lavendar learns the story, he tells Willy King that she must confess, and he is right. Confession in these cases brings happiness. The physician is less able than the minister to anticipate the psychological burdens of wrongdoing.

Gentle, charitable, and realistic, Willy King is a man of ethics and tends his patients with humor and kindness. Although he is the proverbial henpecked husband, he accepts his married life with good humor. He was not, Deland remarks, moved by mere prettiness and so married a woman of common sense. Because Mrs. King is a paragon of housewifeliness, Dr. King's life is in order, his buttons sewed on, his income carefully spent. Martha King is also a moral watchdog of Old Chester, and she makes certain that Dr. Lavendar knows her opinions of his sometimes unorthodox actions. Deland pokes gently at the industrious and serious Martha, who never understands why Dr. King so often drops in to visit Lucy and Horace Shields, to hear piano playing, to play cribbage, or to listen to idle chatter. Martha's very lack of humor provides the reader with a chuckle as she bustles around Old Chester, doing her "duty."

Humor is one of the key elements in the Old Chester stories. Deland often viewed the human condition as a source of amusement. The eccentricities of her Old Chester inhabitants and the comic inconsistencies of human beings are part of the charm of the stories. Miss Mary Ferris, who took to her bed for thirty years after she was jilted, never rises "except on Saturdays when the sheets are changed."[4] In a domestic scene Deland comments that the cook always belongs to the wife if the dinner has gone badly. The fluttering of the Jay sisters when they see a man in tights, the stinginess of William Rives asking Dr. Lavendar to return a stamp, Mrs. Barkley's probings into her neighbor's business are all delightful bits of human reality. The Old Chester gossip when something shocking has occurred reveals as much about the human condition as the crises that are the subject of the gossip.

Deland's primary theme in the stories is the need for personal integrity and individual responsibility, both linked to common sense. Her stories show her belief that men and women can regain a moral life after falling into sin. This belief in people and their ability to redeem themselves from both sin and foolishness became a strong theme in her fiction. Human mistakes in *The Wisdom of Fools* and *Mr. Tommy Dove and Other Stories* are often impossible to rectify. In later stories Deland expressed more confidence in the ability of men and women to see their mistakes, to improve their lives, to be responsible for their own happiness. In the short stories she had left behind those stiff, dull characters from the early novels and wrote about real human beings, weak and strong, foolish and sensible. Her characters no longer spoke sermons; they spoke their feelings.

Bits of Lace, Bits of Steel

Reviewers always praised Deland's stories for their picture of a simpler time in history. But her stories offered more than a nostalgic view of quaint social customs and old-fashioned virtue. She probed difficult ethical problems, and she probed the problems of the woman in a world where woman had only one proper role.

When Deland was writing, opportunities for women were expanding. More women were working; more were attending college. The period of most of her stories, however, offered far fewer opportunities for women. In fact, the only life considered proper and satisfying for a woman was marriage and children. Deland herself believed that a good marriage was the cornerstone of a happy life for a woman.

Marriage is used in many of the stories as a solution to various problems. Women are literally rescued from starvation, oppressive families, and even sin by marriage. Even strong women need this rescue because the world in which they live provides no other choices. The gratitude these women feel when at last a man steps forward to save them is pathetic because it suggests how truly helpless a woman is by herself. When Amanda Gedge accepts William Sprague's offer to marry her, thus saving both herself and her mother from destitution, she cries, "Oh, I *must* save mother! and you are so kind, so very, very kind to think of this way."[5]

When Maria Welwood is faced with poverty after her nephew has lost her income in a business deal, Deland comments harshly on women's inability to earn a living. The question of earning a living is "ghastly," she writes; "it was especially so in a place like Old Chester. . . . It is a wretched enough question even in the great busy world. . . . No one can quite understand the misery, the sick hopelessness . . . but the woman herself."[6] Maria decides to open a school, but she knows, and Old Chester knows, that she will fail. When lawyer Ezra Barkley takes pity on her and proposes marriage, Maria accepts, smiling "through her tears." In "House of Rimmon" Lydia Sampson is rescued from a clerk's job when Reverend William West, touched by her courage, proposes marriage. In these situations a generous man steps forward gallantly, not out of love but out of kindness.

Women had need of being rescued from more than financial disaster. The situation of the unmarried female relative who must impose on a brother, cousin, or uncle and live surrounded by his family is a very uncomfortable one. For these women, marriage brings escape from a second-class status in the community. In "Turn About" Jim Williams marries Netty Brown, young enough to be his daughter, because she is unhappy about being a burden to her uncle's family. "The Unexpectedness of Mr. Horace Shields" ends happily when sixty-five-year-old Horace proposes to twenty-three-year-old Lucy, who is miserable living with her sister's family. In this case, Lucy also rescues Horace from loneliness following his brother's death. Dorothea Ferris is trapped in a drab existence living with her two maiden aunts until Oscar King sweeps her into marriage ("The Promises of Dorothea"). In "Good for the Soul" Bessie is saved by marriage from a life of sin and a shabby existence as a member of a traveling dance troup. Good-hearted Peter Day does not realize that he is rescuing Bessie and giving her a new life.

Marriage often rescues people other than the two who marry. In "Miss Clara's Perseus" when Clara Hale and Fanny Herbert, childhood friends, are being driven to distraction by living together in their middle age, Oliver Ormsby steps in. Fanny is a poor widow and has nowhere to go. Clara is a spinster and wants her old, familiar, quiet life. Oliver would prefer to marry Clara, but she has always refused him. So he marries Fanny, thereby rescuing her from an uncertain future, and he rescues Clara from Fanny's presence in her house. In "The Mormon" Deland shows a dynamic, attractive mother-in-law who has usurped her daughter's place in her son-in-law's life. Augustine is an actor, and Adèle manages his career, travels with him, and introduces him to society while Dora stays home with the baby. Adèle is a happy widow with no wish to marry again, but when old friend Henry Austin, seeing the situation, proposes to Adèle in front of Dora and Augustine, Dora becomes almost hysterical with joy. Adèle suddenly understands what she has been doing to her daughter and marries Henry to save Dora's marriage.

In Deland's world marriage is a sorting out, a settling of events. People are in their proper places with marriage; women are protected; society runs smoothly. She never implies that marriage always brings deep happiness, but she does promise a pleasant contentment if the parties choose wisely. Although she gently pokes fun at industrious Martha King and other ladies who are the moral overseers of Old Chester, Deland is caustic in her criticism of fluttery, helpless women and of men who seem to prefer them. Dr. King is unusual in that he chose common sense when he married. Deland says in "The Promises of Dorothea" that generally "a man prefers a fool every time" (12). Dorothea, Dr. Lavendar says, has no more will than a wet string. Amelia Dilworth is a good woman, but has no mind and is totally helpless with her headstrong children ("Amelia"). Mrs. Price in "An Encore" rules her husband and her father-in-law with "foolish weakness."

Women who idealize their men or the romance itself make mistakes in these stories. Annie Shields so idealizes her husband that she can't see his weaknesses in "The Thief." There are constant misunderstandings because she fails to see Tom Hastings for the rather cowardly and unintelligent man that he is. When she discovers that he copied the poem she thought he wrote for her, she is shattered. Dr. Lavendar tells her that she is the thief, however, because she has stolen Tom's individuality, his chance to become strong. Other women ruin their own chances for happiness because they cling to a romantic ideal rather than seek happiness realistically. Elizabeth Sayre refuses to let Oliver Hamilton propose to her because she idealizes the notion that there must be only one love in a person's life, and she wants Oliver to be true to his wife's memory ("Elizabeth"). When she finally realizes her mistake, it is too late. He has turned to someone else. These women are foolish because they do not look realistically at situations and build their lives on what is rather than what should be.

Deland's stories, however, are also full of strong women who, in contrast to these helpless or foolish creatures, struggle to help themselves, use their intellect, and, in fact, often have to provide balance and strength for their men. Even though some strong women must be rescued through marriage, that is the fault of society, which so closes off options that a woman has no choice. Deland shines a light on the inner strength of women like widow Lizzie Graham who lives in a New England village on a Civil War widow's pension of twelve dollars a month in "The Immediate Jewel." Slightly dotty and nearly blind, Nathaniel May comes to town talking about the invention he is working on—a machine to allow people to talk to the dead. Nat has no money and no home. Lizzie takes pity on him when no one else does. She can't marry him to give him a home because she'll lose her pension, so she tells him he can come and live with her although she knows that her reputation will be ruined. Lizzie chooses between public opinion and kindness to another and has the strength to make the right choice. In "Many Waters" a successful lawyer agrees to admit to an old theft and make restitution only after his wife argues with him and says she will somehow pay it back if he won't. "Sally" shows the generosity and strength of Sally, who sacrifices her personal happiness to care for her family. Her mother is silly and helpless. Her brother is weak and lets her support him. Her sisters expect her to stay home so they can do what they want. Sally is the foundation of the family and, even after she marries, will continue to take care of them. Another strong woman is Rebecca Gray in "An Exceeding High Mountain." She has always lived in the shadow of Robert Gray's beautiful and delicate first wife. When Rebecca learns that the child of that first marriage was not really Robert's, she decides never to tell her husband. She gives up the chance to destroy his memory of his first wife—the memory that has always made her plain and unwanted by comparison. She is strong enough to let the chance go by.

What Margaret Deland was showing was the diversity in women. Her heroines are not all fluttery and helpless; they are not all strong and intelligent. The full range of human qualities appears. Her work with unwed mothers in Boston led Deland, perhaps inevitably, to writing about women who were not respectable. They, too, are not all alike. Some, like Mary Dean in "The Child's Mother," fill their lives with lies. Others, like Bessie Day in "Good for the Soul," take their chance at respectability and build a solid life. "Mrs." Holmes in "R. J.'s Mother" wants to be sure that her son never thinks anything but the best of her. She lives a careful, circumspect life while pretending to be a widow.

It is easier to remember Deland's women than it is her men. Dr. Lavendar and Dr. King are vivid characters, but other men are either dim copies of those two gentlemen or ineffectual parasites, who must draw on the strength of their women.

The Novelettes

Some of the Old Chester stories were really novelette length. "A Fourth-Class Appointment," which appeared in *Mr. Tommy*

Dove and Other Stories, was published separately as a novelette in 1913. The title was changed to *Partners,* and Deland re-edited slightly, but the story of the two women soon to lose their post office remained. From *Old Chester Tales* both "Good for the Soul" and "Where the Laborers Are Few" were published separately in 1899 and 1909 respectively. Deland's stories made popular gift books with the covers decorated, margins illustrated, and full-page prints of key scenes.

Some novelettes appeared first as books and later in collections. *An Encore* (1907) is an amusing story of two elderly people whose elopement forty-eight years before had been thwarted by parents. Now, meeting again, their renewed courtship is being opposed by their children. They elope again and are married by Dr. Lavendar in an orchard. The story appeared later in *Around Old Chester.* Also in that collection was *The Voice,* first published in 1912. The story was based on the Irvingite religion, which Deland had learned about during a trip to England in 1890. *The Voice* concerns an Irvingite who moves to Old Chester and waits for the power to speak in tongues while his daughter finds romance after almost poisoning the man she loves with a potion. The story seems bizarre now, but it is another illustration of Deland's belief that religious fanaticism is destructive to those around the fanatic.

Another novelette about an unusual religion was *The Way To Peace* (1910). While on a stroll, Athalia Hall and her husband Lewis meet an old Shaker. The Shaker community is dying out since the members do not believe in marriage. However, Athalia gets bursts of enthusiasm (temporarily) for nearly everything she sees, and, after a brief visit to the community, she decides to become a Shaker, abandoning her husband without a thought. Lewis faithfully lives nearby, waiting for her mood to change. After two years Athalia does change her mind; unfortunately, it is too late. Lewis has become a Shaker, and now Athalia is the one rejected for religion's sake. This story touches on the theme in *John Ward, Preacher*—a marriage split by religious fanaticism. But the story is also about a silly, unrealistic woman, who feels no responsibility to the choice she has already made and her duty to that choice. Responsibility to duty is a theme appearing over and over again in the short works. Deland labeled individual freedom with no thought of others shallow

and selfish. Athalia's whim is selfish, and her religious fanaticism
disrupts lives and hurts good people.

The dangers and consequences of religious fanaticism remained a lifelong theme for Deland. *The Promises of Alice* (1919)
concerns the pull of several responsibilities on Alice, daughter
of a New England minister. Her mother, disappointed that her
husband never became a missionary, raises Alice to be one.
Alice, who doesn't want to be a missionary, is on the eve of
leaving for China when, fortuitously, her mother dies. The story
continues through complications that either put Alice on the
verge of going off to be a missionary, although she is terrified
at the idea, or put her safely out of missionary work, although
she then feels guilty. Alice is just an ordinary young woman
who wants to marry her sweetheart, but she is trapped by a
childhood promise to her mother, a religious fanatic. Mrs. Alden's unrealistic and idealized dream of missionary work comes
close to ruining her daughter's life. Alice is finally saved by
an unexpected inheritance, which enables her to contribute sub-
stantially to the missionary cause and also be happy in her marriage. Alice is one of Deland's weakest heroines. She can do
nothing to control her own destiny. Her mother represents both
the unrealistic woman and the religious fanatic who creates fantasies that others cannot live up to.

A stronger heroine appears in *The Hands of Esau* (1914), a
slight story about a young man who learns that his dead father
was a corrupt businessman who died in prison. His fiancée knows
the truth and wants him to have the courage to tell her so
there will be no secrets between them. When he keeps silent,
she breaks the engagement. Nina believes that Tom has the
moral responsibility to tell her the truth and give her the freedom to decide what to do. Since he is unwilling to risk losing
her, he proves he is not concerned primarily with her happiness.
The situation is the reverse of "Good for the Soul," in which
the wife does not tell her husband of her sins before marriage.
Since she has led a good life for years and since the truth now
will not enable her husband to make any new choices but will
only hurt him, the stronger decision is to keep silent. The wife's
concern for the husband comes in her silence; the young man's
concern for his fiancée should have come in his revealing the
truth and giving her a choice. Nina is too strong herself to

accept an insecure man for a husband. Her father doubts that she will ever marry.

The best of Deland's longer stories are *The Story of a Child* and three novelettes dealing with women who defy convention, collected in *New Friends in Old Chester* (1924).

A child's mind. *The Story of a Child* (1892) was written in the years between *Sidney* and *Philip and His Wife*. Both of those novels were flawed by unrealistic characters and stilted dialogue. *The Story of a Child*, however, is a tour de force, showing an almost magical ability to enter the child's mind and look at the world from the child's point of view. Dialogue is real; events are real; even more, what is real is also delightful.

The story is a sequel to Deland's first short story, "Mr. Tommy Dove" (1889). In that story elderly druggist Tommy Dove shyly courts rich Jane Temple, who is living with her brother's family in Old Chester for the summer. The romance of Tommy Dove and Jane Temple is distressing to Henry Temple on several counts. He does not think a druggist is a suitable match for his sister. But even more, Jane Temple, as an unmarried woman living in her brother's family, serves them all and her presence makes life pleasant. She plays with the children, cares for her semi-invalid sister-in-law, and entertains for her brother. If Jane were to marry and have her own home, the Temple family would lose her services. When Tommy Dove starts to propose, Henry Temple interrupts and dismisses him. Mortified, Tommy leaves town and does not return until fall, after the Temples have left. Jane at first expects him to return, but then realizes he is embarrassed and accepts the end of her little romance. "Mr. Tommy Dove" ends in misunderstanding and blighted hopes.

The Story of a Child starts four years later. The Temples have returned for a summer, and Tommy Dove has left Old Chester again to avoid seeing Jane Temple. The story, however, concentrates on eleven-year-old Ellen Dale, who lives with her grandmother. Mrs. Dale loves her granddaughter, but she is unable to show her love. She never tells Ellen that she is pretty for fear the girl will become vain. She insists Ellen do chores to avoid laziness, and her choice of clothing for Ellen is old-fashioned. But in all she is trying to bring Ellen up to be a lady of dignity and grace. What she does not realize is that children need both reassurance that they are loved and explanations for why they are to behave as they are directed. When Ellen flings her arms around her grandmother and says, "I love you very much," Mrs. Dale responds with "There, my dear, there; control yourself, Ellen."[7]

Ellen finds happiness in her world of fantasy. When she eats rice pudding, she pretends to be a St. Bernard rescuing stranded travelers, represented by the raisins. That she promptly eats the travelers does not interrupt her fantasy. She makes friends with Effie Temple, a proud little snob who greatly resented Tommy Dove's attentions to her aunt in the earlier story.

The two girls play "martyrs," picking hollyhocks to represent people who will eventually be burned at the stake. Sometimes Ellen crawls into the bread oven and pretends to be a martyr walled up and starving. Imagination creates their entertainment. When the two girls dig in the woods for buried Indians, Ellen pictures what she'll find: "solemn figures lying straight and still within it, figures holding burnished spears, and glittering with gold and gems, and decked with drooping scarlet plumes" (47–48). Margaret Deland describes the games that she played as a child in Pennsylvania, but she is able to do more than merely remember the games. She is able to create the magic moments of childhood when exciting fantasy so easily crowds out dull reality and imagination produces excitement in a minute. The girls' fantasies give them instant escape from adult regulations.

Those regulations annoy Ellen this summer because Effie expresses shock that Ellen must do chores. Ellen thinks her grandmother doesn't love her, and Effie agrees because a loving grandmother surely would not make Ellen set her own tea table or learn hymns on Sundays. "Goodness," Effie says, "I wouldn't be like you for anything" (63). With equal candor, Effie tells Ellen the story of Jane Temple's poor romance, concluding, "And anyway, she can't ever get married; she has to take care of us" (62).

Surrounded by adults, encouraged by Effie, Ellen finds freedom in fantasy. The biggest adventure is to run away. She has thought of it, but it is Effie who sparks the idea into a real plan. "I tell you what let's do; let's run away and be missionaries. You know lots of hymns, don't you?" (64). When the time comes to run away, Effie, predictably, backs out but brings Ellen some cake and eggs (unboiled) for her journey. Ellen trudges away, gets lost overnight, and is miles from Old Chester when she decides that actually living an adventure is not as much fun as imagining it. In the meantime, Effie has confessed, and a general search is under way. The next day Ellen is trudging back in the direction of Old Chester when she meets Tommy Dove, who has left the train at Mercer and is walking the twenty miles back to town. Ellen is so grateful to be found that she blurts out what Effie told her—that Jane Temple was sorry when he went away. Ellen is reunited with her grandmother, and Tommy Dove proposes once more to Jane Temple, mending the broken romance at last.

The depth and range of the child's imagination are fascinating in this story. Also striking is the child's need for openly expressed love, which Deland emphasizes elsewhere. In "Justice and the Judge" Judge Morrison never shows his love for his nephew until the boy is dying. Rachel Dudley's Quaker aunt and uncle are unable to show their love in "At Whose Door?" and the girl is killed in an accident, thinking that no one loves her. The ending in *The Story of a Child* is happier as Ellen and her grandmother both break through barriers and demonstrate their concern for each other.

Deland dedicated the story to her cousin Nannie Campbell, whom she had thought of as a sister. Ellen Dale's thoughts and feelings were Deland's own and the ability to re-create them was one of her special talents. As a portrait of the life of a child, this story is a touchstone.

Old Chester shocked. The last three novelettes that Deland published were "The Eliots' Katy" (1924), "An Old Chester Secret" (1920), and "How *COULD* She!" (1921), collected in *New Friends in Old Chester* (1924). The stories, which are among Deland's best, all focus on women who defy convention to follow their convictions. In "The Eliots' Katy" Deland returns to the unwed mother. Katy McGrath, an English immigrant, illiterate and ragged, arrives in Old Chester after walking the twenty miles from Mercer. She gives no explanation of herself, but tavernkeeper Mrs. Van Horn gives her a job in the kitchen. Katy sends most of her wages to an address in Mercer, works hard without complaining, and keeps to herself. When Mrs. Van Horn's daughter-in-law returns a year and a half later, Katy goes to work for Professor Eliot and his wife. Her hard work and honesty gain her respect, but no one yet knows anything about her. Once a year she visits Mercer for thirty-six hours. Finally, Katy tells Mrs. Eliot that she has a young daughter whom she boards in Mercer. Katy didn't want to marry Lissy's father. "E was a low sort. I wouldn't have demeaned myself to *marry* 'im. Anyway, I never knowed 'is name."[8] Katy's daughter Lissy is the most important thing in her life, and she glows with pride when she talks of the girl.

Mrs. Eliot is shocked at Katy's sin but impressed with her courage. She tells Katy that the Eliots will help with Lissy's education, and she tells neighbors that Katy is a widow, thus giving Katy the freedom to have Lissy visit her.

Katy toils cheerfully for her child, building her little fund for education. Lissy does well in school, but, as she becomes educated, she also becomes embarrassed by her mother's ragged clothes, uncouth table manners, and ungrammatical speech. She tries to disassociate herself from Katy. Her visits become less frequent. When she meets a rich young man at college and accepts his proposal, she tells Katy not to come to the wedding and tells her husband very little about her mother. Katy does not realize that Lissy's coldness is directed at her until she arrives in the college town for a surprise visit to her daughter and her new husband. Lissy hides Katy in a boardinghouse and makes feeble excuses for not bringing her home. Katy understands at last and, in her final sacrifice for her daughter, suddenly lies and tells Lissy that the girl is really the orphan of rich English aristocrats and that Katy was her nurse. Katy has always believed that lying will keep her out of heaven, so she has sacrificed her place in heaven for Lissy's happiness.

The plot is somewhat predictable. The child becomes a snob, ungrateful for her mother's sacrifice, unable to see the beauty in Katy's character. The figure of Katy, however, is a magnificent portrait. She strides through the story, strong and cheerful, plain and ignorant, with the single-minded purpose of raising her daughter to be educated. She is not attractive; she is tall with big hands and feet, broadbacked and heavy. She wears shoes only on Sunday; she eats with a knife; she has worn, roughened hands and blackened nails. But she loves her daughter with complete and fierce devotion, so much that she never quite understands Lissy's distress during the girl's visits, and, in the end, when Katy lies to make Lissy's life easier, she tells herself that Lissy's mother-in-law frightened her into rejecting her mother.

Katy is a figure of animal vitality and raw strength. Her honesty and her daughter are the center of her life. The convention of the rest of the world in dress, in manners, in behavior does not concern Katy even when Lissy criticizes her. Her sexual sin in having a baby without marriage is simply a fact of nature. What is sin to Katy is dishonesty; therefore, her lie to Lissy is the greatest sacrifice she has made in a life of sacrifice—she gives up her hope of heaven. Katy personifies human love without pretense. She is a unique individual.

Another figure of love is poor, middle-aged Lydia Sampson in "An Old Chester Secret." When her landlord's daughter becomes pregnant before marriage, Lydia talks to old Mr. Smith and convinces him to give the girl and her fiancé a big wedding. The couple goes away after the wedding, and some months later Lydia makes a mysterious trip. She returns to Old Chester with a baby, telling neighbors that Johnny Smith is an orphan, and she is caring for him. The Smith family has provided money for Lydia and the boy, but they will not acknowledge the child for fear of scandal. Old Chester gossips are interested in the mysterious child but can get no more details from Lydia, who devotes herself to raising Johnny. He grows into a sturdy boy and one day catches the eye of old Mr. Smith. Mr. Smith grows fond of Johnny and decides to adopt him. Lydia replies that only Johnny's grandfather can adopt him. Because old Mr. Smith will not publicly acknowledge the boy, Lydia keeps Johnny without interference. When the old man dies and Johnny's parents return for the funeral, Mary and Carl Robertson see their son for the first time and become interested in him. To the distress of Lydia, they send Johnny presents and have him visit over the following years. She fears that the natural parents will claim him, but they still cannot bring themselves to acknowledge Johnny publicly.

When Johnny is twenty-three, Mary's desire for her son causes her to blurt out the truth. Johnny rejects her, saying that Aunt Lydia, as he calls her, is the only mother he will ever have. "I won't acknowledge you!" he tells his father. "Stay hidden.

I won't betray you" (192). Johnny cannot forgive his parents' cowardice all these years in allowing Lydia to care for him and to be gossiped about for returning to town with a mysterious child. Dr. Lavendar finally persuades Johnny to forgive his parents and be kind to them.

Mary Robertson in this story did what Katy McGrath would not think of doing: she abandoned her child, the proof of her sexual transgression. While Katy grows magnificently strong through her struggle to provide for her child, Mary grows spiritually weak since she is ashamed to acknowledge her child's existence. Dr. Lavendar explains to Johnny, "She tried to get away from shame by getting away from you. Now she knows that only by staying with you could she really get away from it" (196). The sin here is not the premarital sex but the cowardice in not accepting the responsibility that results.

Lydia Sampson is everything that Mary Robertson is not. Lydia accepts the responsibility of Johnny, risks the gossip of the town, and becomes the real mother. And she is rewarded with Johnny's unfailing loyalty and love. When he hears the truth of his parentage, he is shocked that Mary could allow Lydia to take the brunt of the gossip. Lydia is the figure of strength in Johnny's life. She gambles when she tells old Mr. Smith he can adopt Johnny if he acknowledges him. She is gambling that the old man's pride will protect her, and she can keep Johnny. She gambles again when she lets Johnny visit the Robertsons and be tempted by their wealth. His love for Lydia never wavers. Lydia is tiny, frail, and elderly, but she is as strong as Katy when she battles for the child she loves. The real parents cannot fight her because their pride makes them weak. Lydia, however, is not afraid of disgrace and, therefore, is stronger.

The third strong woman in this trio of novelettes is Rose Knight in "How COULD She!" Rose becomes engaged to Dr. Lyman Holden of Mercer. However, he is physically attracted to flirtatious Lucy Hayes. On the stage to Old Chester one day Lucy maneuvers Lyman into kissing her. He confesses to Rose and is forgiven, but Lucy continues to attract him. When she visits his Mercer office, he kisses her again and says he wants to marry her, knowing as he says it that his passion will eventually fade. He cannot, however, resist her now.

When Lyman asks Rose to release him from their engagement,

she refuses. Since no self-respecting woman would refuse such a request, Old Chester gossips are horrified that Rose would reveal herself as so desperate for a husband. Lyman refuses to see Lucy again and goes away to do postgraduate study. Lucy, frustrated that she can't prevail upon him to break the engagement without Rose's consent, elopes with an old beau. Rose then immediately releases Lyman from their engagement. She has saved him from Lucy, saved him from the unhappiness that he expected to have once his physical desire for Lucy waned. Lyman no longer wants to be free, but Rose insists, "I will never marry anyone, but you least of all" (271). She has saved him from Lucy because she loves him, but she has given up her reputation to do it. She will not marry him. Lyman is too weak to be her husband.

In saving Lyman from a disastrous marriage, Rose sacrifices her position of respect in the community. At first, Old Chester gossips refuse to believe that she will not release Lyman; later they express amazement. Rose, more than Katy, a servant, or Lydia, an eccentric, is a member of Old Chester society. As the schoolteacher, she has the admiration of everyone. Her sacrifice of her reputation is as bold as Lydia's gamble and as selfless as Katy's lie. Rose knows she is right; she follows her own counsel. In doing so, she loses the respect of everyone. Even Dr. Lavendar urges her to abandon Lyman, to let him marry Lucy and eventually be miserable. When Rose finally releases Lyman, the gossips come to her support again: Rose is too fine to marry a weakling.

The women in these stories are of different classes, but they are all strong because they are bold, because they ignore society and do what they, not others, feel is necessary for those they love. None of them is rescued by a man. In fact, the men here cannot be depended on. Katy's lover, Johnny's father, Lyman Holden, all desert their responsibilities. But the women do not. They represent the kind of strong women Deland admired most. These three novelettes, Margaret Deland's last short works, show her faith in the woman of independence, the woman with her own mind.

Chapter Four

The Feminine Ideal

The Women's Building at the 1893 Chicago World's Columbian Exposition represented the first major recognition at a world's fair of the contributions of women throughout history. Although Mrs. Potter Palmer's opening address assured the audience that woman's natural place was in the home, the building itself, designed by a woman and filled with exhibits by women, demonstrated that women excelled in many areas beyond domestic duties. Paintings, murals, a 7,000-volume library, busts of famous women, all focused new attention on woman and her role.

Although the Seneca Falls woman's rights convention had been held in 1848, it had taken well over thirty years for the stirrings of the woman's movement to influence significantly the popular literature of America. By the 1880s, a new type of heroine had begun to appear in fiction. No longer did the heroine simply scream and faint and wait to be rescued by a man; no longer did she passively let herself be directed by a man. The new heroine was physically active, intellectually curious, and determinedly independent. By the 1890s, novels (primarily by women) discussed women's sexual needs, economic independence, educational aspirations, and legal rights.

Margaret Deland was not an ardent feminist. She opposed women's suffrage and believed staunchly that marriage was the cornerstone of a woman's life. She cannot, however, be called an antifeminist because she always criticized women who were helpless, fluttery creatures, unwilling to develop their minds. She insisted that women must use their brains, that they must have sex education, that birth control was essential, and that the "feminine ideal" was due for change. Deland, therefore, was a moderate, fearful that feminism would destroy the family, but pleased to see women actively using their minds and energies.

Selfishness and Sacrifice

After concentrating on short stories for twelve years, Margaret Deland returned to the novel in 1906. During the next ten years she produced her three best novels: *The Awakening of Helena Richie* (1906), *The Iron Woman* (1911), and *The Rising Tide* (1916)—all focusing on women.

Her first successful novel after *John Ward, Preacher* was *The Awakening of Helena Richie* eighteen years later. The skills she had developed during her years of writing Old Chester stories all came into play here as she created vivid, realistic characters and a gripping story of a woman's realization that one's personal morality affects others.

The story concerns a new resident of Old Chester, Mrs. Helena Richie, who has moved into the Stuffed Animal House left vacant by the death of its owner. Helena is beautiful, charming, and quite alone except for occasional visits from her "brother," Lloyd Pryor of Philadelphia. Helena rejects the friendly advances of Old Chester residents, refusing all invitations and preferring to live in seclusion. Dr. William King, while treating Helena's sick cook, is charmed by the quiet, pretty Mrs. Richie, so different from his sensible, practical wife, Martha. When Dr. Lavendar tells him that a seven-year-old orphan needs a home, Dr. King immediately suggests Helena. After some hesitation, Helena agrees to take in young David and soon loves him as though he were her own.

Helena tells Dr. King that her husband was a drunkard who caused the death of her baby twelve years earlier. What she does not tell him is that her husband is not dead but living in Paris. Helena left her husband after her baby's death and went to her lover, Lloyd Pryor, a widower with a young daughter. The two were sure that Frederick Richie would drink himself to death within six months, and they would be free to wed. But Frederick didn't die, and Helena has lived on the outskirts of society wherever she has been, maintaining the fiction of brotherly visits from Lloyd and waiting for marriage to make things right.

Aside from Dr. King, Helena's only other frequent visitor is twenty-three-year-old Sam Wright, who is infatuated with her because she listens (or seems to listen) to his dreams of being

a playwright. Sam's father objects to his son's not settling down
to business and urges him to stop bothering Helena. The young
man is closer to his grandfather, Benjamin Wright, who quar-
reled with Sam's father thirty years ago and has not spoken to
him since. During a chance call on Helena, old Benjamin meets
Lloyd, who is visiting, and the old man accurately assesses the
situation. When Sam proposes to Helena, she tells him that
he is foolish, and he decides to go away to try to get his play
published. His grandfather, relieved that Sam is going away
from Helena, gives him the money for the trip.

Lloyd is pleased that Helena has taken in David because the
boy will keep her busy, and Lloyd will be free to make less
frequent visits. The old passion has dimmed over the years,
and Lloyd is now fearful of destroying the trust his nineteen-
year-old daughter has in him.

At a surprise party arranged by Dr. King so that Old Chester
can get acquainted with Helena, a telegram comes saying that
Frederick Richie is dead. Helena sends word to Lloyd, who
answers that he is going west for six weeks. They will talk when
he returns.

Sam returns to Old Chester, having burned his manuscript
after a publisher rejected it. He tells his grandfather he intends
to propose again to Helena; Benjamin then tells him that Lloyd
is Helena's lover. Sam confronts her, and she confesses, thus
destroying his ideal of her. Later that night Sam kills himself.
Old Benjamin Wright suffers a stroke when he hears of Sam's
death and is unable to talk. Helena's secret is safe now, but
she feels that she is responsible for Sam's death. She has always
believed she could live apart from society with her own code
of behavior, but now she begins to see that society depends
on a common ideal of moral behavior. By her actions she has
violated the ideal and disrupted society.

Lloyd finally writes to Helena and says that their original
intent to wed no longer is convenient. His daughter, Alice, at
nineteen, is not likely to want a stepmother, and he is afraid
she will discover the truth of their relationship. Nevertheless,
he tells her that he will fulfill his promise if she holds him to
it. Helena is crushed at his obvious lack of love, but she ignores
her pride and writes that they must be married. She is convinced
that she can never feel free of guilt, can never feel like other
people until she is married. She breaks down and tells Dr. King

the truth. His shock at learning that she is not what he thought is another blow to her, particularly when he tells her that she must give up David—she is not fit to care for a child.

When Lloyd arrives, he says that he will live up to his promise but points out that David, who has known him as Helena's brother, obviously cannot be part of their family. Helena cannot bring herself to give up David and so breaks with Lloyd. She sends David to visit Dr. Lavendar while she tries to decide what to do. Dr. King, who obviously has been in love with Helena, urges her to tell Dr. Lavendar the truth and to give up David. At last, Helena, not knowing what else to do, confesses to the minister. She wants to move away and take David. Dr. Lavendar suggests that she gave up Lloyd for David out of a selfish desire for her own happiness, not out of concern for David. She admits that she cannot do the boy any good and realizes that she has always thought only of her own happiness.

With Dr. Lavendar's help Helena arranges to move west and begin a new life. On the day she is to leave, the old minister gives David back to her because she is no longer thinking only of her own happiness, and she understands that her personal actions are a part of the moral structure that holds society together. She is now a mature woman who can accept her responsibilities to others.

The theme of *The Awakening of Helena Richie,* and a lifelong theme of Deland's, was based on German philosopher Immanuel Kant's categorical imperative: that is, society is held together by moral laws, and one's actions cannot be those that, if done by all, would destroy society. Individual freedom must never infringe on the common good.

Helena herself knows she is outside society. She does not want to meet Old Chester people; she refuses to have supper with Lloyd at Dr. King's. She will not accept someone's hospitality and play a lie. She is aware that Lloyd has segregated his affair with her from all other parts of his life. He dislikes even showing a picture of his daughter to Helena and tells her that Alice's great charm is "her absolute innocence."[1] The comment is "like a blow in the face." Helena has lost Lloyd's respect over the years and become a casual incident to him, totally separate from his life.

Helena thinks that marriage will change everything—erase

her sin and make her respectable. She believes, as she and Lloyd told each other years before, that her life is private and has no effect on anyone else's life. Her awakening must be to the fact that her actions are not entirely her own, that they do affect others, and that she is not only outside society but she is threatening it. Years before she had believed Lloyd's assertions that mere convention had no hold on them. Now she begins to see that Lloyd was merely reassuring her, that he himself had never believed that.

Helena has spent her life passively drifting. "All my life I only wanted to be happy," she says (29). She has always selfishly tried to satisfy her own desires before anything else. Deland here draws a sympathetic yet critical picture of a woman who must move from self-delusion and a preoccupation with self to realistic evaluation of herself and her personal responsibility.

Helena's first shock of recognition that her actions affect others comes when Sam Wright kills himself, not because she spurned his love but because she shattered his ideal of her. The distinction is important: Helena had no responsibility to love Sam, but she did have the responsibility to live within the moral structure of society. At Sam's funeral she realizes she has been undermining the society she always claimed had no connection with her private happiness. Her "excuses of her right to happiness . . . crumbled and left her selfishness naked before her eyes" (250). She could not be totally separate from society. She could not think only of personal happiness.

Helena's first response to recognizing her blame for Sam's death is to demand marriage. Deland comments that Helena "mistook marriage for morality" (250). Although Deland believed in marriage, she does not imply here that it confers morality on anyone. Morality comes from within the individual. Helena must accept personal responsibility for her life, must recognize her selfishness, must act out of concern for others. When she gives up Lloyd to keep David, she is still acting selfishly. Only when she admits to Dr. Lavendar that she cannot do David any good and gives him up has she really awakened to her responsibility to place others ahead of her own happiness, to accept duty as part of her life. She is on her way to becoming a new person. When Dr. Lavendar gives David back to her, he is showing her forgiveness, telling her that a new life is possible.

The novel moves Helena from being the kind of woman Deland disliked to being the kind of woman she admired. At first Helena is fluttery and helpless; she can't cook or sew; she eats candy, takes naps, and putters ineffectually in the garden. She is charming and lovely and makes men feel protective. Dr. King falls in love with those qualities but, like Sam, also sees in her an ideal of purity that does not exist. When Helena moves toward self-recognition, she becomes more realistic. Finally, she is strong enough to sacrifice her own happiness for the happiness of someone she loves. In the end Dr. Lavendar tells her to study Hebrew or Russian to exercise her mind, the last step in developing into a worthwhile woman.

Every character in this novel is a realistic portrait of a complex human being, reflecting both the strengths and weaknesses of character. Dr. Lavendar is the wise minister, stern but forgiving once he sees Helena's recognition of her sin. He shows his belief in her new moral sense when he gives David to her. David reflects the child who is alone, cautiously offering his love, but not wanting to give too much to these people who may leave him as he has been left before. When at last he gives Helena his "forty kisses," he gives her his trust, a responsibility Helena must be strong enough to handle. Lloyd Pryor represents a certain masculine morality. He has a strong sense of personal honor. He is taking responsibility for the debts of his father's old firm although he is not legally bound to do so, and he is willing to marry Helena because he gave her his word, and he always keeps his word. Unlike Helena, however, Lloyd knows that marriage will not erase their affair or suddenly make them moral. He sees a great barrier between Helena and his daughter Alice: Helena is no longer socially or morally acceptable as a stepmother to Alice. Lloyd Pryor is not an evil man; he is the man who, having had the woman easily, now finds her less alluring, less amusing. Lloyd sees Helena's beauty as faded. The sin has changed his view of her.

However, to Dr. William King, Helena is lovely, flower-like. The doctor is a simple man falling in love with the beautiful and mysterious Helena, her helplessness appealing to him, her beauty seeming to reflect her goodness. His complete trust in Helena's goodness and then his horror at her confession help Helena to face the truth about herself. She has shattered Dr. King's ideal as well as Sam Wright's ideal. That Dr. King can continue to see her, to advise her, shows his maturity in contrast with Sam's. All three men had loved her, and all three found their love gone when she failed to support the ideal of sexual morality. Margaret Deland did not excuse her heroine because she was in love or because her lover had convinced her that conventional morality did not matter; it was part of Deland's belief in individual responsibility that Helena must see that she has been mistaken and that she alone bears the blame for the results of her actions.

The Wright family, with three generations of men unable to express their love for each other, unable to forgive until the death of the youngest at last brings the father and grandfather together, shows the tragedy of pride. Sam is unstable, given to wild extremes of emotion. One rejection by a publisher causes him to destroy his play. The shock of Helena's sin sends him easily to suicide. Because he has been mistaken, he believes there is nothing left to do but destroy himself. His excess of emotion reflects the absence of emotion in his father and his grandfather, whose anger has frozen into a thirty-year silence broken only by death. In both extremes, pride is the controlling force leading to waste of human life.

This novel is one of Deland's best—a portrait of a woman caught in society's double standard of morality. Helena's awakening to the weakness of her position and to her foolishness in accepting Lloyd's assertions that they are above morality leads to her development as a woman. At last she sees herself in relation to society, and she is strong enough to sacrifice, strong enough to depend on herself.

Smoke and Duty

The Iron Woman (1911) begins three years after *The Awakening of Helena Richie*. Helena, after a stay in St. Louis, has moved to Mercer with David. Their neighbors are Sarah Maitland, owner of the Maitland Iron Works, and her son Blair and stepdaughter Nannie. Helena's landlord is the works' manager, Robert Ferguson, who lives next door with his niece Elizabeth. The children all play together, bringing the elders together because of the children's friendships.

Helena remains quietly beautiful, a perfect lady, refined and elegant, devoted to her son. In contrast is Sarah Maitland, tall, ugly, rough, and awkward, who runs her ironworks with a zest for the rough world of business, a delight in the swirling smoke of the works. Successful at business, Sarah is less successful as a mother. She loves Blair and Nannie but cannot express her love nor can she see what they need. Nannie is afraid of her rough personality, and Blair is spoiled by having everything he wants. The only way Sarah can show her love is to heap material goods on her children. She cannot give them her time; that is devoted to her business. She does not know how to listen to them, be friends with them; she has no sense of them as people.

The children grow up, and both Blair and David fall in love with Elizabeth. When David finishes college and is in medical school, he and Elizabeth become engaged. A teenage flirtation with Blair meant nothing to Elizabeth—it has always been David she adores. Blair, amid much carousing and much debt, finally graduates from college. His mother, disappointed in her son, bails him out of debt and difficulties and thinks raising his allowance is the answer to his irresponsibility. Blair travels in Europe, takes art courses, and at last comes home to a job in the works. Sarah ignores the fact that Blair is not interested in the business; she gives him an inflated salary and plans for his future as owner.

Robert Ferguson awkwardly proposes to Helena, but she refuses him because of her past. She is moving to Philadelphia to be with David, who will intern at a hospital there. His marriage to Elizabeth must wait two or three years until he is settled in a practice.

While David is in Philadelphia, Elizabeth inherits a small legacy, enough to support a couple for two years. She writes to David, telling him that she wants to be married at once. David's pride won't let him live on his wife's money even for a short time, so he refuses. Elizabeth is mortified; her temper flares; and, one afternoon when she chances to meet Blair who still loves her, she impulsively elopes with him.

The marriage horrifies all the families, and Elizabeth regrets her impulse the next day. She begs Blair to let her go, but he refuses, thinking he will make her love him. They live in tense confrontation, Elizabeth frozen into a feeling of emptiness. Sarah grimly cuts her son off from her money—he must support his wife by working. She changes her will to leave Blair only a small allowance. In addition, Sarah begins a trust fund, which she intends to give to David when he finishes his internship so that he can build a hospital in Mercer.

One year later Sarah is injured in an accident at the mill. She dies, leaving the certificate of deposit for David's trust fund in Nannie's hands. In her confusion at the end, Sarah had written Blair's name on the certificate. After Sarah's death, Nannie forges her stepmother's signature, believing that Sarah had forgiven Blair at the end and meant the certificate for him. Robert Ferguson, knowing Sarah's original intention, figures out what must have happened. However, Blair refuses to believe the money was meant for David and will not give it back.

After three years of silently enduring her marriage, Elizabeth cannot tolerate Blair's attitude about the money, and she cannot convince him to give it up. She disappears, going to David in the middle of the night. The two reaffirm their love, and David urges her to stay with him, telling her that Blair will have to divorce her then, and they can marry. Helena, guessing where Elizabeth has gone, arrives to stop them. She blurts out the story of her past, telling Elizabeth that she, too, had once believed a man's promise that he would never tire of her if she gave him what he wanted. The shock of Helena's confession separates the lovers, and Elizabeth returns to Blair, resigned to keeping her commitment. She tells Blair that she can never feel more than friendship, but she will stick to the bargain she has made. After another six months Blair can no longer endure Elizabeth's quiet withdrawal and tolerance, and he offers to divorce her.

Helena hopes Elizabeth will refuse Blair's offer and stick to her duty. But Robert Ferguson thinks David and Elizabeth will marry when they can. He proposes again to Helena, but she refuses again—she will never feel that she is free to marry.

The Iron Woman is a continuation of the story of Helena and David but, even more, it is a reworking of Deland's theme of personal responsibility—no one can do as he wishes if those actions done by all would destroy society. Again, there is individual happiness versus commitment to duty—to marriage. Even though this marriage has ruined lives and made all concerned miserable, Deland's view that marriage cannot be dissolved just to make people happy remains unshaken. The ambiguous ending—the reader cannot be certain that David and Elizabeth will eventually marry—adds a strength and realism to the novel, lacking in the ending of *The Awakening of Helena Richie* where the happy resolution seems to give a simplistic assurance that, if one repents, one will be happy. In *The Iron Woman* David and Elizabeth are grimly resolved to do what is right and give up happiness. At the end the reader sees a possibility for future happiness, but Deland does not resolve the issue and implies that, even if Elizabeth and David eventually do wed, they will always be marked because they went against the ideal of marriage. This more realistic ending—unresolved as lives are unresolved—makes *The Iron Woman* a stronger novel than *The Awakening of Helena Richie.*

The story focuses on the younger people, but all the characters are developed into complex individuals, and Sarah Maitland, the iron woman, is one of the greatest portraits in American fiction. A woman of vast heart, vast strength, vast determination, Sarah strides through the novel completely divorced from standard feminine roles, completely herself. She gives orders to her men, "a big, heavy woman, in a gray bag of a dress that only reached to the top of her boots . . . her gray hair was twisted into a small, tight knot at the back of her head, and her face looked like iron that had once been molten and had cooled into roughened immobility."[2] She sees the greatest beauty in usefulness and, thus, cannot understand Blair's passion for art. Production, labor, commerce—these are what excite her. In her independence, her unconventionality, her satisfaction in her work, Sarah loses the chance to be a good mother. Blair is embarrassed that his mother is so unfeminine, and Nannie is terrified of her. Sarah loves her children but cannot understand them and has no patience with personalities weaker or more hesitant than her own. She thinks that giving Blair more money will keep him out of debt. Strong herself, she makes her children weak by never giving them responsibility for their own lives.

Sarah's death is one of the most gripping scenes in Deland's fiction. Mr. Denner in *John Ward, Preacher* quietly fades into a peaceful acceptance of his death. But Sarah Maitland rages and struggles against her fate. At first, her injury does not seem serious but, as her condition worsens and her mind slips in and out of lucidity, she marshals her strength for her final battle. She refuses to stay in bed—bed is where one dies. She roams the house. When she is weaker, she lies on the floor of the dining room propped up by pillows, vowing that she is getting well, alternating between delirium and her old strength. "She seemed like a great tower falling and crumbling in upon itself" (334). Although the plot focuses on the romance of David and Elizabeth, Sarah Maitland dominates the novel, her failures as a mother paling (perhaps more than Deland intended) next to her success as a dynamic businesswoman and her personal strength.

Representing beauty, charm, and feminine concerns, Helena is a contrast to Sarah. Yet she is stronger than in the previous novel. In the end she is a woman, saving Elizabeth, another woman, from the man who would ruin her—Helena's own son. Helena feels the genuineness of the emotions of the lovers, but she has learned that men tire of women they have ruined, that once reputation is lost it cannot be regained, and that David is no different from other men who whisper to women that their love is special. Her concern for another woman is stronger than her mother love. Elizabeth gets the courage from Helena to stick to her duty, to retain her self-respect.

It is the women who control the events in this novel. Sarah and Helena influence and struggle with the younger generation; Elizabeth impulsively marries Blair, changing three lives, and then holds the future of those lives as she stoically accepts responsibility for her act. Even timid Nannie, to save her brother from being cut off without funds, forges Sarah's signature after she dies, setting in motion the struggle over money that causes Elizabeth to flee to David.

The men look to the women for guidance. Although repulsed by his mother and what she stands for, Blair is not willing to train himself to make a living independently. He lives on his mother's money, not caring about the opinions of others. David, honorable and respected, will abandon all that respect in a moment when Elizabeth comes to him. " 'Right' is being together!" he tells her (436). His mother must force him to make the moral choice he can live with, must stop him from ruining Elizabeth as Helena had been ruined. Robert Ferguson, a friend to Sarah but dominated by her, in love with Helena but confused by her, enraged by his niece's behavior but never able to handle her, has virtually no influence on any of the women in his life.

The Iron Woman comes alive in its characters, particularly in its women, and their struggles with their own passions, their own needs, and the claims of society. Deland touched the best of realism here, what she once called "this great, patient, pathetic, divine human nature."[3]

Suffrage and the New Woman

Margaret Deland often lectured on her opposition to women's suffrage, but her third best-selling novel in the years before World War I had a suffragist heroine and presented some serious views of women's concerns.

The Rising Tide (1916) is set in Mercer and is Deland's only truly contemporary novel. Frederica Payton is a "new woman." She smokes; she swears; she marches for suffrage; she runs a sometimes successful rental agency. Fred, as she is called, espouses every argument as well as every cliché of the feminist cause. "Girls don't have to knuckle down any more and 'obey'; they can . . . break away, and support themselves . . . this life servitude that men have imposed upon women of looking after the home, is done, *done,* for good and all!"[4] She shocks her elders with her frankness, saying about her severely retarded brother that he ought not to have been born. Fred blames her father's sexual misdeeds for Mortimore's condition and talks viciously of the need for health certificates for men before they marry. Mrs. Payton, relatively content since her abusive and dissipated husband died, has devoted her life to her son and to jigsaw puzzles. Fred, however, refuses to have anything to do with Mortimore, and she upsets her mother with frank comments about birth control, sex education, inactive women, her father's sins, and innumerable other topics revolving around the oppression of women.

Fred's closest friend is her cousin, Laura Childs, who agrees with Fred's opinions but is not "so hideously truthful as Fred, and her conceit was not quite so obvious" (38). Another friend is Howard Maitland, heir to the Maitland Iron Works, who professes great admiration for Fred's activities and opinions. He finds her ideas "simply stunning." Howard's interest in col-

lecting and cataloging shells is dismissed by Fred as insignificant,
but Laura is always thrilled with his talk of his collection and
new finds. So Howard admires Fred who has a "man's brain"
(69) and falls in love with Laura who appreciates the importance
of his interests. Arthur Weston, trustee of the Payton estate
and family friend, admits the truth of much of what Fred says,
but wishes she were more feminine, less aggressive, less upset-
ting. Fred amuses Arthur; he tries to help and advise her; he
argues with her; finally, he realizes that he is in love with her.
However, the twenty-one-year difference in their ages seems
too large, and he dismisses the idea of ever telling her. Moreover, Arthur, like everyone else, expects Fred to marry the
admiring Howard Maitland. While her relatives are kept busy
recounting each new (and shocking) activity, Fred works at her
rental agency and makes speeches to women factory workers,
telling them the ballot will bring them higher wages. She further
shocks everyone when she rents a summer cottage and makes
plans to stay there overnight with only a servant.

   In a quiet moment one day Fred realizes that she is in love
with Howard, and she takes his compliments—"I'd rather talk
to you than any man I know" (68)—as signs that he returns
her love. But before she can tell him of her feelings, Howard
goes off on an expedition to hunt shells in the Philippines, leaving Fred to continue her suffrage activities. Because she is so
happy to be in love with Howard, Fred takes Arthur's advice
and spends more time trying to make life pleasant for others.
She tries to cheer up the maid Flora, who has been disappointed
in love, and she is kinder to her mother.

   When Howard returns after nine months, Fred immediately
invites him to her lake cottage for supper. That evening she
tells him that she loves him and proposes marriage. His shock
and embarrassment show Fred at once that she has made a mistake. After a bit of awkward conversation in which the two
try to pretend that their relationship can continue as it was,
Howard decides to drive back to town. He and Fred then discover that Flora the maid has drowned herself in the lake. In
a frenzied drive to take Flora's body to a doctor, Howard and
Fred are able to forget their personal feelings. Later, however,
Fred thinks with mortification about the proposal and realizes
that she was wrong, that women cannot take the initiative in

romance, that such aggressiveness cheapens women and makes the men indifferent. The man values only what is difficult to achieve. Since the permanence of the relationship is crucial to the welfare of any children, the women must make commitment attractive to the man through her reluctance. He must struggle to win her. It is Fred's first realization that some of her opinions may be wrong, that feminism cannot wipe away all the traditional attitudes. Deland comments that it is the business of the "new woman" to "discard the absurdities, but keep the beauties and dignities" (239).

Howard proposes to Laura immediately, and Fred is a bridesmaid at their wedding, a smile frozen on her face. After the wedding Fred is involved in a strike by women rubber workers, giving speeches and urging the women to keep up their cause. Laura won't march in parades because Howard doesn't approve, but she offers to accompany Fred, who is speaking to strikers at a rally. When police arrive to clear the sidewalks, Fred scuffles with a policeman, and suddenly she, Laura, and an Italian worker are on their way to jail. After several frantic phone calls Fred locates Arthur and Howard, who arrive to bail the women out. Howard is in a rage that Fred has exposed Laura to such an experience, and Fred suddenly sees that he has never truly supported her ideas, that she has never truly understood him. She is stunned at her mistake.

Arthur manages to keep the newspapers from printing the story of the arrest; he also settles the charges so Fred and Laura don't have to appear in court. Fred continues to work for reform, but she tells Arthur that she is not certain any more that the ballot will free women: "I'm sort of discouraged about what we can accomplish" (280). Her youthful arrogance is gone; she does not feel young any more. Impulsively, Arthur reveals his love for her, and Fred quietly suggests that they marry. He protests because of his age and the fact that she does not love him. However, Fred says that she is fond of him and he is her best friend. She would be quite content to marry him. When the engagement is announced, her friends are surprised but also much relieved—Fred has a man to guide her at last.

The Rising Tide is a novel of ideas rather than plot or character. Deland wanted to criticize both sides of the feminism issue, and she succeeded. Fred and her opinions reveal much of what

distressed Deland about feminism. Articulate and overly confident, in her eagerness to reform the world, in her conceit that
she has all the answers, Fred has no sensitivity to others, no
sense of any responsibility to those around her. She accuses
her mother of being a "parasite," living on money from her
husband—a man she disliked and feared. Mrs. Payton's "duty"
should have led her to leave her husband, not to endure him.
Mrs. Payton represents the older generation, helpless and mindless. She is devoted to an idiot son but not even able to care
for him herself; she must hire a twenty-four-hour nurse. Mrs.
Payton fills meaningless roles, but she is lonely and she would
like to understand her daughter if she could. Fred delights in
shocking her, criticizing her for a way of life that is, after all,
what Mrs. Payton was brought up to accept. Fred believes in
"truth" and rather enjoys offending everyone with her comments. She is crude often for the sake of being crude, and it
is this abandonment of taste and tact that Deland presents in
this novel as one of the weaknesses of feminism.

Fred's self-confidence in her opinions leads her not only to
widespread insult and inconsiderate behavior but also to personal humiliation. She misreads people. She thinks that Howard's admiration of her daring means that he admires her ideas.
In fact, Arthur, who argues with her, agrees with her far more
than Howard does. Her most serious error comes when she
violates tradition and proposes to Howard. She is surprised at
the depth of her own humiliation when he rejects her. For
the first time she analyzes the position of men and women.
She sees that male pursuit and female hesitation help keep the
relationship permanent and form a protective environment for
the children. Deland is warning here that if the "new woman"
abandons what lures the man, if she becomes the pursuer, she
will lose the protection for her family. Society, built on the
family, will be shattered.

Fred learns that she cannot completely handle her own life.
When she is arrested, she turns instinctively to Arthur for help—
she turns to a man. Arthur's rescue of her, her mistake in proposing to Howard, her loss of confidence in her ideas, all these
turn Fred back toward the more traditional female role. Although she is content with Arthur, although she trusts him,
she will not abandon all her beliefs. She has, however, lost

her radical feminism. She is more moderate, reflecting the position Margaret Deland had on feminist issues.

Deland illustrates the extremes of the feminist question here in Fred and her mother. Mrs. Payton is a useless creature, wasting her days, dedicating herself to an ideal of duty to her son—an ideal devoid of common sense. She tells Fred that Mortimore is the head of the family and refers often to Aunt Adelaide, who devoted her life to an idiot brother. Mrs. Payton's idea of duty is senseless. She contributes nothing to society. However, Fred, until she learns better, refuses to admit that she has any duty at all. What Fred comes to see is that doing her personal duty, fulfilling her responsibilities to her family and friends, will not interfere with her independence or her work for women's rights. Fred must learn to apply her common sense to her duty, to blend the two so that what she does has value both for the feminist cause and for those who need her.

Laura Childs represents more acceptable limits of feminism. She chides her mother about getting exercise and casually teases her father, but she defers to her father's objections to parades and rallies. She is active in clubs, takes design courses, and talks about reform and the ballot, but she lacks Fred's abrasiveness. When Laura marries Howard, her family becomes the center of her life; other issues remain interesting but become less important. Although she usually defers to Howard's judgment, she tells him that intellect has nothing to do with sex, but she also tells Fred that a woman doesn't know life until she has a baby.

The novel shows that many of Fred's opinions are correct. Fred is admirable in her energy, her concern for working women, and her determination to get social justice for women. Her belief that women should work rather than be parasites on the labor of man is valid, and Arthur Weston agrees with her about the value of work in women's lives and to the nation. He admits that invention has changed the home; work there no longer consumes all of a woman's attention. A woman has a right to more stimulating activities, and it is already true that if all women returned to the home, the economy would suffer.

Arthur also admits to the truth of Fred's charge that men have created a standard of conduct that keeps women weak and ignorant and leaves men free to indulge their passions.

Women must know about birth control, about sexual diseases; women must not tolerate their men's immoral activities; women must not blindly depend on men's chivalry; women must have the knowledge and strength to make their own moral choices. "It's the double standard that has landed us where we are; it has made men vile and kept women weak," Fred tells Arthur, and he knows that she is right (139). Arthur is, in fact, suitable for Fred as a husband because he is intelligent enough to acknowledge when she is right.

The Rising Tide is a compendium of the issues that women were discussing in the years before suffrage was granted. In Deland's view both sides were right—and wrong. Fred is admirable but absurd, gallant but crude, brave but foolish. In the end she seems to retreat to woman's traditional role as wife. But the novel shows clearly that the days of the fluttery, helpless woman were ending. The "new woman," with all of her mistakes, was a creature of brains, wit, and self-determination.

The End of Dora

In 1902 Margaret Deland wrote a short essay, "The Passing of Dora," for *Harper's Bazar*.[5] "Dora" referred to the completely brainless and helpless first wife of David Copperfield, and Deland was glad to note that such women were ceasing to be in the majority, ceasing to represent the feminine ideal. In most of her work, but particularly in the three novels of this period, Deland presented a picture of what she saw as the changing feminine ideal—a woman with intellect, strength, and independent moral judgment. But this "new woman," as Deland saw her, must also retain her charm and dignity, her love of home and family, and her deference to a husband who deserves that deference. Fred Payton will fit that ideal when she settles into marriage. Arthur is attracted to her precisely because of her independence and her brains. He is a man who can give Fred both guidance and freedom because he is more thoughtful and more sensitive than most men. Deland said often that the changing feminine ideal required a change in men as well. They had to give up the "Doras" and accept women as capable and intelligent partners.

Margaret Deland, however, does not say, as many popular

women writers did, that marriage to a mature, understanding man is the answer to all problems. Helena Richie can become an independent responsible person only when she realizes that marriage will not absolve her sins, will not make her respectable. The "new woman" needs the combination of an independent mind and the acceptance of social responsibility rather than a husband who will make her decisions for her. That Deland understood how difficult such a combination was to achieve is evident in the struggles undergone by the women in her novels. Helena must abandon her selfish seeking for personal happiness, must give up what she wants most, before she can become a woman worthy of respect. Sarah Maitland never quite manages all her responsibilities, in the home and on the job. She can never combine her duty to her business with her duty to her children. Her business comes first, and Deland regards that as a failure. Elizabeth ruins several lives before learning a commitment to duty, before learning that absolute freedom infringes on others. Fred must be demoralized and embarrassed before she can feel true sympathy for the hurts of others and understand that radical change will undermine society. For many women, such as the older generation in *The Rising Tide,* there is no hope of attaining the new feminine ideal. They are "Doras," useless to themselves and vulnerable to others.

In several essays of the period Margaret Deland wrote about her perceptions of the "new woman." She applauded the emergence of the more active woman, although she warned of the possible dangers. She wrote in the *Independent* that "The excitement of the new sense of ability, which we have treated rather like a new toy, is sobering into the realization that economic independence brings great spiritual responsibility." Once women accept that responsibility, however, "We shall look at this Woman in the Market Place with love, and admiration, and confidence, and envy!"[6]

Chapter Five

Failed Marriages

In the years between *The Rising Tide* (1916) and Margaret Deland's last novel, *Captain Archer's Daughter* (1932), the world changed radically. World War I left a generation of people disillusioned with their elders' apparent failure to prevent war or achieve a lasting peace. With that revolt against the politics of the past came revolt against the morals and standards of the past.

The age of the flapper arrived and with it Prohibition. Hemlines rose; bathtub gin enlivened parties; motion pictures set patterns of behavior and created "stars" to emulate; Ford autos filled the highways; radios blared in living rooms. Women voted and entered the workforce in ever increasing numbers. A group of writers in Paris became the voice and symbol of the "Lost Generation." Novels discussed new moral codes—or a lack of them—and suggested that all ideals were dead.

The Scopes Monkey Trial brought evolution into casual conversations; Freud's theories added the terms "neurosis" and "Oedipus complex" to the national consciousness. *Mein Kampf* was published in Germany; Lindbergh flew the Atlantic; and the stock market crashed. The Great Depression of the 1930s brought an end to the frenzied search for happiness. More important became the search for a job.

Margaret Deland's last three novels reflect some of her own uncertainty in these years. She continued to set her work in the past, in familiar places, but other things changed. Her husband had died in 1917, and Deland had entered wholeheartedly into war relief activities, writing a series of propaganda pieces. When she turned again to the novel, her work revealed that, like her contemporaries, her perspectives, her certainties, were shifting. The last three novels all deal with failed marriages— mismatches that become painful unions. Unlike her earlier works, in which Deland stressed the ideal of duty, the refusal

to abandon a commitment, these novels examine the deteriora-
tion of a union and the inevitable unhappiness of people trapped
by their mistakes. Divorce was still not an answer for Deland,
but the confidence that doing one's duty would bring at least
contentment was missing.

Jealousy and Infidelity

Set in Mercer, *The Vehement Flame* (1922) opens with the
elopement of nineteen-year-old Maurice and thirty-nine-year-
old Eleanor. The couple's only family, Maurice's guardian
Henry Houghton and Eleanor's aunt Mrs. Newboldt, are
stunned at the news. The age difference is the most obvious
potential problem; however, the Houghtons and others quickly
see a more serious one. Eleanor is lovely but empty. Maurice
fell in love with her singing voice and believed that her long
silences were mysterious. But the Houghtons see at once why
Eleanor is silent. "Eleanor's mind," Henry Houghton says, "is
exactly like a drum—sound comes out of emptiness!"[1] The
Houghtons reconcile themselves to the marriage and welcome
Eleanor to the family. Eleanor, however, dislikes eleven-year-
old Edith Houghton, partly for her youth and partly because
Maurice enjoys playing with her. Eleanor wants to be the only
person in his life. Seeing him happy excites her jealousy; she
wants him to think only about his love for her. *"I* don't want
anyone but you," she pouts (79).

The newlyweds settle into a house in Mercer where Maurice
begins his career as a real estate agent, and Eleanor decorates
a nursery, hoping a baby will come. Unfortunately, domestic
life is uncomfortable because Eleanor knows nothing about running a house or directing a cook, and she makes little effort
to learn. After two years they move to a boardinghouse so
that Maurice can get a good meal. Eleanor hates the boardinghouse because she wants Maurice all to herself, and he enjoys
chatting with the other boarders.

While out rowing with Edith one Sunday, Maurice assists
three people whose boat has overturned. One boater is Lily
Dale, who is pretty but obviously a prostitute. Eleanor's constant
tears and jealousy finally cut into Maurice's patience. One day
after a quarrel he goes for a walk, encounters Lily, and strikes

up a conversation. Months later, after another quarrel, Maurice visits Lily, who has given up the streets and now has a job as a salesgirl. She cooks a delicious dinner for him and entertains him with amusing stories. Bored and irritated with Eleanor, Maurice is unfaithful with Lily a while later. He feels guilty but is by now angry with himself for being such a fool as to marry Eleanor. Still, he resolves to stick by his bargain and does not see Lily again.

However, in a few months Lily writes that she is pregnant and needs money for the baby when she must stop working. She is thrilled to be having a child and intends to keep it. Maurice grimly accepts his responsibility and begins a life of deception, giving Lily a small steady amount of money. Lily rents a tiny house and takes in boarders; Maurice visits occasionally, vaguely repelled by his small son, Jacky, the product of his sin. Maurice's only pleasant relationship is with Edith, who attends boarding school in Mercer, but his pleasure in Edith's company excites Eleanor's jealousy, and she complains constantly.

When Jacky is six, he contracts scarlet fever. Lily sends a frantic telegram to Maurice, and, since he is not home, Eleanor reads it. She says nothing but bitterly begins to realize the truth and see her own failings, her constant selfishness. Maurice, arriving home later, finds the resealed telegram and rushes to Lily. He arranges for a hospital room and pays all the expenses. The boy recovers, and for the first time Maurice is interested in him. He begins to visit Lily regularly and gradually feels his responsibility to Jacky as a person not just a symbol of sin. He realizes that he loves the boy and begins to worry about his schooling and his future.

Jacky is nearly nine when Maurice finally tells Eleanor the truth. She forgives him for the lies and joins his interest in the boy, wanting to see him, wishing she and Maurice could raise him. For the first time in years they are almost happy together because they have a mutual interest. Eleanor believes that Jacky will save her marriage, that if they can adopt him she will have nothing to fear from Edith. She can't quell her jealousy of the young woman because she senses that Edith and Maurice have grown to love each other over the years. In a fit of anger, she accuses Maurice of being in love with Edith, and he suddenly realizes that Eleanor is right. Eleanor goes to Lily and asks her to give Jacky up, but Lily refuses.

Upset, thinking that it would be best for all if Maurice were free to marry Lily and terrified because Edith has admitted that she loves Maurice, Eleanor tries to drown herself. But she becomes frightened of the water and retreats, arriving at Mrs. Newboldt's soaked and shivering. She is put to bed with a fever. Ill as she is, Eleanor quarrels with Edith again, telling her about Maurice's son, telling her that Maurice will never marry her. After having Maurice bring Jacky to her bedside, Eleanor dies. For a while Maurice considers marrying Lily but then tells the Houghtons that he will have more influence with her regarding Jacky's upbringing if they are not married. Although the Houghtons feel Maurice should not marry again, Edith insists they have a right to happiness and says she will marry Maurice.

The Vehement Flame is Margaret Deland's strongest attack on the helpless woman, the clinging vine, the "Dora" of her essay twenty years before. Her authorial voice is harsh and critical as she comments, "There is no man who is so intelligent that the Clinging Vine makes no appeal to him," (48). Deland seems, indeed, to have modeled some of Eleanor's story after the story of David Copperfield's child-wife Dora in Charles Dickens's classic novel. Although Eleanor is mature where Dora is young, they have the same foolish minds. Eleanor's lack of intelligence makes the age difference in her marriage doubly important since the appeal of the older woman is most commonly her mind, her knowledge, and variety of experience. Eleanor has nothing to say; she sits in "sweet, empty silence" (45). She is dull, without humor, and never understands Maurice's need for other people, for activity. She tells him over and over that she wants only him, and she expects that he will want to be only with her. Her demands for all his attention are childish, and when Maurice finally calls her "silly," the glow of his boyish love starts to fade. Eleanor's constant tears and headaches bore him, and her inability to appreciate anything outside of her narrow world deadens his interest in her. It is not really the age difference but Eleanor's lack of intellectual maturity that sends Maurice to Lily and makes him curse his own stupidity for marrying Eleanor. However, Eleanor's age accentuates her defects. She is the mindless girl grown into the mindless woman, and Deland shows clearly that what might perhaps be amusing in a girl is boring in a woman.

Like David Copperfield's wife, Eleanor is not only nonintellectual, but also helpless on the domestic scene. "Any cooking takes brains," Deland remarks (83). Eleanor not only cannot learn how to cook, she cannot even give directions to a hired woman. They must move to a boardinghouse in order to get a good meal. Although she tries, Eleanor cannot begin to learn how to manage. She can only enjoy her music and complain that Maurice neglects her. Her dog, Bingo, reflects her jealousy when he snarls at anyone who is close to his mistress. He dies when his mistress dies, just as Dora's jealous dog, Jip, died when she did. Both Dora and Eleanor on their deathbeds talk to the women they know are in love with their husbands. But unlike Dora, who gently asks Agnes to care for David, Eleanor feels only the fury of her jealousy. She reveals Maurice's infidelity because she hopes Edith will turn away from him.

Deland's theme is the corrosive nature of jealousy, the flame which eats away at the marriage. Although the Houghtons and Mrs. Newboldt warn her, Eleanor cannot curb her jealousy, and her frequent outbursts over any interest Maurice displays in anyone or anything destroy his love and finally isolate Eleanor into what she feared—a woman alone, forgotten by her husband. She is incapable of being interesting or of developing interests. She can only try to hold back Maurice, to keep him to herself. Maurice goes out to dinner, to the theater, to see friends alone. Eleanor never wants to go and never wants to share him, not understanding why Maurice is not content to sit in a room with her. Eleanor represents the kind of woman Deland found most reprehensible—dull and helpless—the opposite of Fred Payton or Helena Richie.

In contrast to Eleanor, Lily Dale the prostitute is cheerful and lively. She is frank about her past, but when Maurice visits her, she is excited about being "straight." Maurice's adultery has little to do with sex; it represents his contentment in Lily's comfortable presence. She does what Eleanor cannot do: she feeds him and entertains him. The sex itself surprises Lily as much as Maurice. But Lily is anxious to be a respectable and an independent woman after Jacky's birth, and she rarely asks Maurice for anything. Her respectability becomes "a deep satisfaction to her" (209). She adores her son, and her fierce determination to have full responsibility for him convinces Maurice that he can influence her more as a friend than as a husband.

"So long as she thinks she has the upper hand, she'll be generous," he says (375). Deland creates in Lily a friendly, amoral little animal.

It is Edith who personifies Deland's ideal woman. She combines Eleanor's gentility and morality with Lily's lively energy and curiosity. Eleanor's jealousy focuses on Edith because Maurice finds her interesting. Edith's brains terrify Eleanor as an enemy she cannot fight, and Deland tells the reader that Eleanor did not have the sense to try to develop Edith's qualities in herself. When Edith accepts Maurice's mistake and his duty to Jacky and defies her parents' wishes to marry him, she demonstrates the mature love that Eleanor could not give. Yet Edith is strangely uninteresting in this novel, perhaps because she so obviously represents the ideal new woman of physical health, lively intellect, and generous heart. She has no complexities.

Eleanor as the empty-headed woman has no complexities either, and one of the weaknesses of this novel is that the major female character fails to excite our admiration or even arouse our hatred. She is only boring, and, like Maurice, the reader has had enough of her long before the story ends. The most interesting woman is Lily who, in her casual morals, her fierce mother love, her cheerful nature, her quick anger, shows the range of human emotions.

The mismatch in this novel results from the fantasies of youth. Maurice, an impulsive college freshman, dreamily worships a woman with a golden singing voice. He calls her "Star." Eleanor is a woman with a "mind as immature as his own" (7). She dreams of love on a desert island, not realizing that real love cannot survive in such isolation. The day comes when Maurice outgrows freshman fantasies and knows bitterly that he has been a fool.

Deland was accused by readers of making the adultery in *The Vehement Flame* attractive because Eleanor so clearly fails as a wife. However, Deland is showing the development of maturity in Maurice through his redemption of his sin. The adultery never gives Maurice any pleasure. He is at once overwhelmed with self-disgust and shame; the shock of his own ability to slide into adultery eliminates any chance of a recurrence. He ages perceptibly and yearns to confess to Eleanor, but, because she is obsessed with her fears of losing his attention,

he cannot face the scene he anticipates. A life of constant deception wears at him—every lie seems to inflate his self-contempt,
to tighten the trap he feels himself in. Since Lily makes almost
no demands on him, Maurice could drift away if he wished,
but he accepts his responsibility for Jacky. His first thought when
he sees his son is "How nasty!" (149), and for years he avoids
seeing the boy when he visits Lily. However, during the scarlet
fever crisis Maurice is the only one Jacky will allow to carry
him to the ambulance, and the father feels the first real tug of
parenthood. Maurice becomes aware of Jacky as a human being,
not just as a symbol of his own folly, and he moves toward
his first mature love for another person. His decision on whether
to marry Lily is based on what would be best for Jacky.

Maurice pays for his sin with ten years of agony, lies, and
shame. He will, in fact, continue to pay in the future whenever
he clashes with Lily's ideas of how to raise Jacky. *The Vehement
Flame* is a bleak look at people caught in their mistakes and
paying for them with years of regret.

Reason and War

The last novel that Margaret Deland set in Old Chester was
The Kays (1926). A New Englander and a member of the Chapel
of the True Followers, Agnes Kay is regarded as "a hard, good
woman,"[2] with a granite, inflexible determination, rooted in
the supreme confidence of being right. She is nondemonstrative,
caring for her son Arthur and carefully teaching him her belief
in reason, but never responding to the child's need for affection
or for a mother like other mothers. She embarrasses him by
refusing to wear hoop skirts, by cutting her hair short, by being
different from other Old Chester mothers. Practicality, not fashion, is her guide.

Agnes Kay has shocked Old Chester by refusing to conceal
the fact that her marriage is a failure. When Arthur was born,
Agnes received a letter revealing George Kay's past sexual involvement, and she ended his rights as a husband, saying he
also had no right to his son. George sleeps in a room off the
library and never goes upstairs. Thus, George does not know
that the crazy woman in the attic, whom Agnes has cared for
since Arthur was a baby and whom George has never seen, is

not a relative as Agnes has implied but is his discarded mistress, gone mad after George's marriage. Because George is director of the state lottery and Agnes believes gambling is wrong, she refuses to use any of his money for Arthur or herself, having the cook prepare two meals—one rich with meat and dessert, the other plain and meager. She and Arthur must live on her small inheritance. The boy also is not allowed to accept any presents from his father; he often goes threadbare, further shocking Old Chester. Even Dr. Lavendar comments that Agnes Kay would give a fox to her son, thus outdoing most Spartan mothers. Agnes cares nothing for his opinion or for any other opinion in Old Chester. "Reformers," Deland comments, "are never pleasant to live with. . . . the egotism of idealism is not only tiring, it is antagonizing" (73).

George Kay, a big, handsome, amiable man who enjoys whiskey, cigars, and laughter, accepts the failure of his marriage and travels a good deal, staying away for months at a time. He is frustrated by the way Agnes raises their son and is afraid the boy will be a coward because Agnes tells Arthur that fighting is always wrong. Further worrying his father, Arthur learns to sew and takes the pledge against liquor. George hopes that Arthur will yet show a spark of "manliness."

Arthur grows up scorned by most of the other youngsters. His only friend is Lois Clark next door, who plays with him and defends him. She, too, believes he is a coward but generously feels that he can't help it and likes him anyway.

Arthur is eighteen when the Civil War begins. Old Chester rallies to the Union cause, even Dr. Lavendar saying that war is sometimes "an abominable necessity" (87). George Kay organizes a company for the young men, but Arthur refuses to join. He believes in the South's right to secede and further, "A Christian can't fight" (95). His refusal to enlist damns him in Old Chester as a coward. Only Lois remains faithful, and the two pledge their love even though Lois is only sixteen. Mrs. Clark has two sons going to war, and she refuses to let Lois see Arthur. When one of Lois's brothers is killed, Mrs. Clark takes Lois to Washington to do hospital work. Meanwhile, Arthur works as a clerk in Mercer, ignoring the harsh criticism of Old Chester residents. However, when George tells his son that there may be a job in the civilian corps, Arthur eagerly accepts the offer.

Although Agnes objects because Arthur will be helping others to kill, Arthur rejects her argument; he must serve in some way.

While he is away, an old enemy starts the rumor that Arthur is selling donated supplies to soldiers for personal profit. When the war ends, Arthur discovers that Old Chester believes the rumor, but he refuses to deny it, stubbornly saying that it doesn't matter what anyone thinks, echoing Agnes's belief that no explanation is ever owed to others. Dr. Lavendar tries to persuade Arthur to deny the rumor, saying that Arthur's reputation affects more people than just him. Even Lois begs him to deny it, but Arthur refuses. He is sure she understands his reasons, not realizing that Lois, too, believes the story but forgives him because she loves him. Arthur and Lois elope because both mothers oppose the match, Mrs. Clark because she has lost two sons in the war and Agnes Kay because Lois doesn't "reason."

When George Kay returns to Old Chester, he denounces the lie about Arthur and says that he will hunt the man down and make him retract his story. But when Lois hears his plan, she begs him not to stir things up. Arthur realizes then that Lois has always believed the stories about him—she has never understood his beliefs; she has only loved him. Stunned, he dashes out of the house. At the same time, Mary is near death after twenty-one years of living as a madwoman in the attic. In the turmoil of calling for Dr. King, George enters the attic and sees her for the first time. As Mary dies, George realizes that all these years Agnes has taken care of his former mistress. When Agnes realizes that Lois believed the rumors about Arthur, she is sure Arthur will never be able to forgive his wife. But at last, near morning, Arthur returns to Lois to try to build a life with her.

The Kays generally was called a pacifist novel when it appeared. Clearly, by 1926 Margaret Deland was no longer a believer in war. One of the most active supporters of World War I, she had written narratives from France, exhorting Americans to wipe out the Germans. But in this novel, ten years later, she labels the calls to war, "glib sanctities of patriotism, the cheap braggings as to America's greatness" (102). In Arthur's conflict between his intellectual assessment of war as stupidity and his emotional pull to join his fellow citizens in the conflict, Deland shows the strength of the two forces. She does not condemn those who follow the call. Dr. Lavendar supports Lincoln's position and the need to preserve the Union. But the strongest argument in the novel comes from Agnes Kay, who catalogs the nation's previous wars as robbery and murder rather than battles on the side of God. "If we lived in South Carolina, wouldn't we think it righteous to fight the North?" she asks (86).

Deland's authorial commentary is strongest in this novel when she asks why war is so compelling. Why does "youth so eagerly rush to the arms of death" (96)? None of the Old Chester residents, she assures us, really knows what war is about. The glory fades as the Old Chester men return maimed or fail to return at all.

The Civil War provides the background for the clash between cold reason and hot emotion, but the focus of this novel is not truly on war and its tragedies. The real clash between reason and emotion is illustrated most vividly by the worst marriage to appear in any of Deland's novels.

The mismatch here is extreme and bitter. In Agnes Kay, Margaret Deland created a stunning portrait of fanaticism and the self-righteousness that accompanies such extremism. Although Deland attacked religious fanaticism throughout her career, Agnes Kay is her most intimate portrait of someone driven by the assurance of being absolutely right. Agnes's fanaticism is all the stronger because it is based not only on religion but on reason. She relies on her intellectual assessment of events and the resulting intellectual decision that she makes. She objects to war because it is against God, but also because it is stupid. She rejects social conventions and contemporary values as worthless if they are not reasonable and practical. Her violation of Old Chester standards is complete. Her dress gives her the label "Mrs. Clothespin." She ignores the opinions of all others, even those she must surely respect. Others do not rely exclusively on reason as she does; therefore, their opinions do not matter. She feels free to make it clear to society that her marriage is a failure at a time when no lady would indicate such a thing. She joins the Pennsylvania Society for the Suppression of Lotteries even though her husband manages the state lottery. She refuses to have sexual relations with him after hearing of his indiscretions before marriage. She refuses to use his money for herself or her son. Agnes's idea of what a wife owes an immoral husband is, Deland remarks, "sixty years in advance of her time" (24). As an independent woman, Agnes is admirable for her integrity, but chilling in her rigidity. There is a wide range in the importance of her actions. Rejecting war or protesting a state lottery may reflect deep moral convictions, but refusing to wear hoop skirts does not rank on the same level. Agnes's total nonconformity causes Arthur much suffering, but she does not care. Even as an adult returning from the war, he wishes that she would wear hoops. Her rigidity in refusing to accept or even consider others' opinions isolates her from society, a fact that causes her no distress. Old Chester knows that Agnes Kay is good, but "nobody liked her" (26).

It is the rigidity, the absolute reliance on her own ideas that creates the fanaticism that grates on others. Agnes Kay is hard. She tells Arthur about forgiveness, *"If you are kind to an enemy, you cannot hate him"* (37). But Agnes herself has no forgiveness. Her devotion in caring for the insane woman once her husband's mistress appears to be a reflection of her belief in loving one's enemies. However, she can tend the madwoman in a blaze of sacrificial self-righteousness. Mary is mad; therefore, Agnes need never really deal with her on a realistic level. Her grim "forgiveness" does not extend to her husband, with whom she would have to deal realistically. She shuts George out, relegating him to the first floor, cutting off his influence with his son, isolating Arthur and herself behind her smug certainty that nothing George does is worthwhile. Agnes can sacrifice comfort, friends, and love to stand by her convictions, but she lacks the Christian forgiveness to give a second chance to anyone who has violated her code. Thus, she represents a reason that is arid, untempered by human emotions, and she is unable to forgive others for their human weaknesses.

In contrast, George Kay is all emotion and sensuous pleasure. Old Chester knows that "Kay was profane, that he loved the ladies, and that he drank more wine . . . than St. Paul advised" (23). And everybody likes him. Sometimes hotheaded, before his marriage he fought a duel and killed a man. He was a major in the Mexican war, and when the Civil War comes, he responds to the war emotion, reflecting the patriotic excitement that sweeps a populace. However, George can never sustain anger. He is alternately angry at Arthur's acceptance of his mother's ideas and hopeful that the boy will prove he is not truly like Agnes. George is mortified when Arthur says he will not fight, but he senses his son's struggle and offers to arrange civilian work.

The union of Agnes and George is empty. They live in the same house but apart. They eat at the same table but different meals. They are so completely divorced that George is unaware of Mary's true identity although she lives in his attic. Mismatched in intellect and emotion, Agnes and George live primarily in silence, struggling on occasion for influence with Arthur, although George knows that Agnes has the upper hand. In spite of his mother's influence, Arthur does admire his father for the very energy and emotional drive that Agnes abhors.

The very differences that kill the marriage are what attracted George to Agnes. He was fascinated with the mystery of her mind "bolted and barred against his simple thought" (130), and he responded to the challenge to melt her icy calm. But Deland says that the icicle was really crystal which does not melt but stays hard and cold. Only the death of Mary gives Agnes and George a glimmer of understanding for each other. He is stunned to realize the burden Agnes has carried all these years, and he appreciates her courage. Agnes, at the same time, realizes that now she has no one who needs her. She may have forgiven Mary, but she has never forgiven George, and she suddenly hopes that Arthur does not become as hard as she is.

Arthur, like his parents, has entered into a mismatch. Lois loves him but doesn't understand any of his values. When he realizes that they understood nothing about each other, that Lois believed the lie about him, he says that he will not return. When he does return, he shows for the first time that he is George's son as well as Agnes's and that he can reject reason and offer forgiveness.

The Kays is Deland's last major statement about the far-reaching dangers of fanaticism. The vanity of self-righteousness is mirrored in Agnes's rigid, unbending nature. Arthur suffers as a boy because of her indifference to outside opinion; when he marries, his indifference to opinion causes Lois suffering.

His ability to forgive is what may save him from the fanatical hardness of his mother.

The mismatched union of Agnes and George Kay is the most bitter in Deland's fiction. In *John Ward, Preacher* and *The Vehement Flame* Deland ends the marriages through death, but George and Agnes are given no such escape. They have wasted years and will waste more.

New England

Margaret Deland's last novel and the only one she set outside the Old Chester–Mercer area was *Captain Archer's Daughter* (1932). Mattie Archer is the quiet, twenty-nine-year-old daughter of retired sea captain Robert Archer. Living in a Maine coastal town, Mattie is a model of propriety and daughterly devotion.

When his ship runs aground at Bowport, handsome Captain Isadore Davis calls on Captain Archer and stays to dinner. Mattie for the first time in her sheltered life feels the fierce pull of sexual attraction. Isadore is "as elemental as a flame . . . as vulgar as the honest earth."[3] When he sails four days later, Mattie sails with him. They are married in Portsmouth, and Captain Archer swallows his feeling that Isadore is the "devil's seed" and tells the town he is very pleased.

The first months for Mattie on board ship are charged with a vivid excitement she has never experienced before. She stops reading her Bible; she learns to smoke; she drinks champagne; she is caught up in the delight of physical love. But when Mattie tries to expand the relationship to include a spiritual and intellectual union, Isadore gets bored. "She slops over, like all the rest of them," he thinks (81). The end comes when she gets pregnant. Neither wants the child, but Mattie, as the woman, has the burden of carrying it and cannot escape the restrictions of motherhood. When it is time for the baby to be born, Isadore takes her to a nursing home in Barbados.

Mattie realizes that Isadore intends to leave her and the baby. He refuses to consider traveling with an infant, and she cannot leave it. "No decent woman will desert a baby," he tells her (89). In a fury, Mattie says she will never live with him again. Isadore quietly says that she will keep her word on that.

When Mattie's son is born, Isadore is already at sea. Her anger subsided, Mattie waits in Barbados, sure that he will return and planning to leave the boy to go with him when he comes. It is Isadore she loves—and despises for deserting her. Although Isadore sends money, he never answers her letters pleading with him to return.

When Cap is twelve, Mattie receives word that Isadore has died. Soon a letter comes from a woman in one of the port cities that Mattie and Isadore had visited on their honeymoon. The woman asks for support for her daughter and encloses proof that she and Isadore were together. Mattie's rage blots out all reason; she throws away all the jewels Isadore gave her and sends all her money to the other woman. Now destitute, Mattie and Cap return to Maine to live with Captain Archer, who adores his grandson immediately. Mattie slips into a fog of memories, rarely leaving the house, doing her duty as a mother but feeling no affection for Cap, unable even to return to her old routines with her father.

Cap grows up happily in Bowport. He makes special friends with Joe Casey, a lobster fisherman, and plays with young Bess Casey. He also plays with Jane Richards, whose grandparents summer in Bowport. When Cap is nineteen, he falls in love with Jane. Both families are very pleased, but Jane's grandparents refuse to allow a formal engagement for a year while Jane travels to Europe.

When the year is up, the Richards prepare to announce the engagement, and Captain Archer gives Jane her engagement ring, a fabulous emerald from his Asian travels. Cap insists that Jane visit the Caseys and become friends with them. Jane politely endures a visit, making light conversation while eating doughnuts at the kitchen table. Later she quarrels with Cap, saying that he cannot expect her to be friends with the Caseys—they are not in her class; she is not comfortable with them. When he continues to insist, Jane furiously throws her ring at him and says she'll never speak to him again.

Cap decides that she will keep her word on that. He suddenly realizes that he really loves Bess and rushes back to her to propose. They can't get married without permission because Cap is underage, but when they ask Mattie for permission, she rouses from her lethargy and goes with them to sign the papers.

For Mattie it is a reenactment of her own elopement. For Captain
Archer it becomes a reenactment of his old mortification and
a betrayal of his friend, Jane's grandfather. But the old man
resolves to welcome Bess into the family.

Captain Archer's Daughter splits into what could have been
two novelettes. Deland attempts to unite the two halves through
Mattie, who wanders like a ghost through Cap's story, and
through repetition of events. The quarrel between Jane and
Cap mirrors the quarrel between Mattie and Isadore, and Cap,
like his mother, elopes impulsively with someone the old captain
does not believe suits the family. But these devices do not make
a unified novel.

The first half of the novel—Mattie's story—is an intense picture of a woman's response to the power of sex. A proper young
woman of 1890 suddenly feels the "scorch" of a physical attraction she has never before imagined and abandons her home
within four days. That sexual attraction gives Mattie life and
excitement: "This was the first time her barren mind had been
fertilized by emotion" (70). The first weeks on Isadore's ship
are all emotion, all hot love. "The only thing that mattered
was that life was quenching the thirst of all her arid years!"
(71). When Isadore deserts her, Mattie says she hates him, but
for twelve years she thinks of nothing but him, waiting for
him to return, planning to abandon her child the instant he
comes back. Her only happiness has been that brief period of
her marriage. His death ends her hatred, and she grows tender
with memories, telling herself that she was to blame because
she let him think she couldn't leave her child. Even discovering
his unfaithfulness does not destroy her obsession with him; she
retreats into fantasies of love.

Like the other marriages in Margaret Deland's last trio of
novels, Mattie's is a mismatch. The sexual attraction is fierce
on both sides, but Isadore Davis is a man of the world in contrast
to Mattie, who has virtually no experience with men. His passion, as it has in the past, burns out—Mattie is, after all, like
all women. He is realistic. Mattie wants their love to go "beyond
the glory of physical love to the greater glory of spiritual love"
(80), but Isadore finds her attempts tiresome. He has had women
everywhere; they are all the same, and he has no interest in
their minds. The mistake he has made in marrying Mattie does

not bother him much; he abandons his wife as soon as he can. Mattie, however, spends the rest of her life reliving the happy time and flailing herself because she thinks he left because of the child.

If Margaret Deland had ended her story with Mattie's return to Maine, she would have had an intriguing novelette, a study of the force of sexual passion in an inexperienced woman. Unfortunately, the second half of the novel becomes a simple and quite ordinary romantic story. Jane and Bess are both stock types rather than developed characters: Bess is the sensible, honest, lower-class girl, Jane the slightly frivolous, slightly snobbish, upper-class girl. Cap echoes the impulsiveness of his parents rather predictably.

The interest of the second half lies in the portrait of the coastal town. Bowport is probably based on Kennebunkport, Maine, Deland's beloved summer home. The social classes of fisherman, summer resident, and permanent resident are reflected in Cap's romances, but most clearly through the three old men—Captain Archer, the wealthy, retired sea captain; Henry Richards, the wealthy, upper-class, summer visitor; and Joe Casey, the Irish lobster fisherman. Although urban summer residents do not generally mingle with the permanent residents, over the years Captain Archer and Henry Richards have become friends. Jane's romance is acceptable to her grandparents because Captain Archer is as wealthy as they are, and they are acquainted with his family tree. Both men respect Casey, but there is a barrier between them that all three understand and support. All are horrified when the young people cross that barrier. In the novel's final scene the three men confront each other as the fisherman tells the two upper-class gentlemen that the granddaughter of one has been jilted and the grandson of the other has eloped with the Irish girl: "—actin' like his father!" Casey says grimly (308).

While Captain Archer is not personally religious and often quotes his own grandfather who said, "nobody who is Somebody looks down on anybody" (24), he has the nineteenth-century Protestant abhorrence of marriage with a Catholic. "A Papist— in my family!" he groans to Henry Richards. Richards reminds him, "Well, Archer, Mr. Casey doesn't want a Protestant in his family. When it comes to objections, he objects on the ground of faith, which is more than can be said of you" (312). The unsuitability of Cap's marriage strikes both men, but Casey is equally upset that Bess would elope without a proper church wedding. The fisherman speaks for them all when he says, "We three, under our clothes, is just alike. . . . We feel the same way about this business—our young ones has give us a lot o' trouble. But we've got to stand by the little fools" (310). This scene of the three old men facing disappointment and joined in pain over the younger generation is Deland's best moment in the second half of *Captain Archer's Daughter*. The scene reflects her respect and affection for the people of the Maine she had loved so long.

The Last Fiction

Margaret Deland's last three novels differ significantly from her earlier fiction. Although she had dealt with the mismatched marriage previously, her earlier treatments had focused on the question of duty to commitment. The characters had to face their responsibilities to the marriage bond and support what Deland believed was the basis of society—the family.

In the last novels, however, that responsibility is not the issue. Deland focuses here on the bitter lives and wasted years of those who choose the wrong partner, those who choose in the first heat of passion. Although Mattie's marriage is brief, her life is spent in fantasies, and is wasted precisely because she can never understand that she was in a mismatched union. Maurice and Eleanor also suffer for years, Maurice because he bitterly knows he has made a stupid mistake, and Eleanor because she doesn't know and can't begin to understand what Maurice needs. And George and Agnes Kay live isolated from each other, both knowing they are mismatched, communicating only when they clash over their son. Margaret Deland does not rescue these people from their mistakes—they must live with them. Even Maurice, freed at last from Eleanor, will always struggle with the residual problems from his marriage. Although in much of Deland's work marriage had represented a sorting out of events and settling of problems, that is not true in these novels. The marriage is the problem.

The second major shift in these novels concerns the emphasis on men. In earlier works Deland's men tended to be replicas of Dr. Lavendar or rather standard types, playing supporting roles to the women. In these books, however, the men become the focal characters. *The Vehement Flame* becomes Maurice's story, his struggle with sin and its aftermath. He is the focus for the reader, as Deland shows his growing maturity, his developing love for his son. George Kay is a complex and realistic human being, angry at himself for marrying Agnes, eager to have his son emulate and love him, believing in the passion and excitement of life. Arthur, too, is important as the struggle between emotion and reason is acted out in his life. In *Captain Archer's Daughter* Deland devotes one half of the book to the story of Cap's growing up and romance, again an unusual emphasis on the masculine character.

The third major shift involves Deland's women. In past work the women were the focal point, struggling to survive, to gain independence, to deal with moral issues. In these last novels, however, the women are either standard types, such as Jane Richards and Bess Casey in *Captain Archer's Daughter,* or they reflect a particular extreme that is not very admirable. Eleanor in *The Vehement Flame* represents the stupidity of the helpless woman, a type Deland had always found repellent; she bores the reader as she bores her husband. Agnes Kay, a thin-lipped unforgiving woman, is the fanatic, secure in her righteousness, superior to those more human and less certain of what is true. Like the citizens of Old Chester, the reader may respect her, but cannot like her. Mattie Archer represents the unreasoned force of human passion. Deland had long advised moderation in all areas, saying people must find the strength to sort through passions for the truth, but Mattie reflects only the blinding power of emotional reaction and the danger of losing one's life to such emotion. Sympathetic at first, the reader grows weary as Mattie clings to an unrealistic dream.

The endings of these novels also offer less confidence than earlier novels did that all will be well in the future. Perhaps Deland in her seventies no longer believed that readers needed that sugary promise.

Chapter Six

Observations and Memories

Margaret Deland's reputation today must rest primarily on her fiction. During her career, however, she wrote a great deal of nonfiction in a variety of forms. She began her career writing short poems and continued to publish occasional verse for over twenty years. She also wrote numerous essays, giving her advice on both domestic matters and the issues of the day. Her two autobiographies were her last writing projects, recording not only her life but also her era. Deland's nonfiction writing reveals her lifelong curiosity about everything her society had to offer.

The Poetry

Margaret Deland began her writing career with greeting card verses for a Boston card manufacturer. Her first published poem, "The Succory," appeared in *Harper's New Monthly Magazine* in 1885. Her only collection of poetry, *The Old Garden and Other Verses,* appeared in 1886. The book, bound in patterned cloth and, therefore, attractive as a gift, proved extremely popular. Deland picked out new cloth for each succeeding edition, and *The Old Garden* continued to be issued as a holiday gift book to the end of the century. Other poems, such as *A Summer Day* (1889), were sometimes issued as holiday gift pamphlets.

Deland's poems were generally short, both rhymed and un-rhymed. She was not innovative in poetry. The pieces are typical nineteenth-century sentimental verse, and she tended to use set phrases. A young girl has "ruddy cheeks and smiling lips," the cows have "gentle eyes," the grass is "bright with dew."[1] Many of the poems in *The Old Garden* are what she called her "flower poems": "The Pansy," "The Clover," "The Blue-Bell," "The Morning-Glory." Others are categorized as "Nature" poems, but there is little difference—"The Wild Rose," "August Wind," "The Golden Rod," "Spring's Beacon." The "Love

Songs" in the collection mirror the style of Deland's favorite poets, sixteenth-century British writers Robert Herrick and John Suckling: "On Being Asked by Phyllis for a Picture of Love," "A Lover to his Mistress," "Sent With a Rose to a Young Lady."

The children's poems are not much different from the adult poetry in word choice or style, but "Bossy and the Daisy" and "The Dance of the Fairies" offer charming images of the sort to amuse children. One of the poems, "The Waits," tells of children greeting Christmas Day. This poem was still being reprinted in magazines for the holiday issues nearly thirty years after the first edition of *The Old Garden.*

Deland continued to publish occasional verse for another twenty-five years, primarily for *Harper's Monthly.* More flower poems reflected her lifelong love of gardening and flowers. Others, "Words, Words, Words," "Whence These Tears?", "Sunset on the Alleghany," continued her sentimental poetry in the vein of Herrick. Fiction, however, offered possibilities for exploring what she considered to be major themes, and poetry became a break from the serious writing she was doing.

The Essays

Other nonfiction that Deland published over her long writing career varied. She wrote occasional reviews, pamphlets for causes she supported, and essays on virtually anything that interested her. *Florida Days* (1889) was a travel book written specifically for the holiday trade. Originally available in three different leather bindings with colored plates, it is a collection of narrative essays that do not really present travel information or reflect Deland's own travel experiences. Instead, she collected information about the St. Augustine area and presented bits of history about the Spanish conquerors and Catholic missionaries. She also described the physical landscape and the local inhabitants, rather harshly saying the Cracker population had "vacant minds" because of the swamps and the solitude.[2] Written during the first flush of her literary career, *Florida Days* is a narrative, paraphrased from encyclopedia entries and packaged to serve as a "coffee table book."

Because she began to write essays after her literary reputation had been established with *John Ward, Preacher,* she published in the larger magazines, including *Harper's Bazar,* the *Indepen-dent, Ladies' Home Journal,* the *Atlantic Monthly,* and *Woman's Home Companion.* Several of her essays on a variety of topics were collected in *The Common Way* (1904).

Margaret Deland's essay style is direct and often personal, particularly in her pieces giving advice. At other times she uses the editorial "we," implying that the reader and Deland agree on the point being discussed. She also frequently makes use of fictional techniques, often creating a scene, characters, and dialogue to illustrate her point.

The majority of her pieces over the years offer advice. "Jon-quils,"[3] for example, suggests how to organize an annual flower sale for charity, as Deland did for years in Boston. Several essays on Christmas giving suggest that people abandon the frenzied struggle to find expensive gifts and instead give something like food or flowers that will convey the thought and then vanish. Her own social class becomes obvious in essays in which she suggests how to handle servants fairly and how to train them.

Her essays on moral questions or essays giving tips for satisfac-tory living are so varied that we can probably assume she not only enjoyed advising readers on everything from old age to gardening but also felt qualified to do so. Much of her advice centers on what she perceives as weaknesses of women: a ten-dency to criticize others, fear of altering traditions, sacrificing personal desires, and spoiling loved ones. Her essays on aging stress the need to keep up with the times and understand the new generation. "We must be able to see the value and the hope in ideals radically different from our own."[4] Deland often mentions her respect for young people and their refusal to fol-low blindly their elders' "poor old ideals."[5] The "truth" of the younger generation may be harsh, she says, but it is honest.

Only a few essays are about writing. She cautions young women to get some experience of life before trying to write. In a four-part series for the *Independent* she calls entertainment the fundamental purpose of the novel and qualifies that by insist-ing on truth in emotion. "Books which show the honest com-monplace of life show also its beauty."[6]

Deland's opinions and her essays on the question of women's suffrage have already been discussed. Although she opposed suffrage as such, she was quite aware that women were entering the work force and that the "new woman" was here to stay. She advocated increased sex education to protect girls from mistakes. She also writes sympathetically in "Aunts"[7] of the unmarried woman who has to live with relatives because she lacks independent means. In "A Deep-Seated Trouble," Deland responds to an article by Thomas Nelson Page in which he describes the isolated and narrow lives of women living in rural areas and advocates more cultural opportunities for Southern mountain whites. She suggests birth control to ease the burdens of those women. Men and women should realize that it is "a crime against society to bring into the world a child for whom they could not provide the two necessities of life—namely, *education and health.*"[8] Increased exposure to the arts, she comments, will not solve the problems of rural women.

Margaret Deland's World War I activities inspired a group of essays collected in *Small Things* (1919). The pieces give her impressions of the courage of the French people and the spirit of the Americans who had gone to fight in Europe. The narratives make no attempt to be analytical or unbiased. She is frankly on the side of the Allies—the Americans are wonderful and show no fear; the French are heroic but dull; the Germans are not quite human. She is unabashedly patriotic, saying America's destiny was to save the world. Her frequent quotations of Americans and the French support her stereotypes so strongly we must suspect she used her fictional talents to create them. She repeats the common atrocity stories—cutting out tongues, ripping babies out of wombs, making women register at the bureau of free love—apparently believing without reservation all that she heard in Paris. Most of these essays were published in 1918 in *Woman's Home Companion,* some after the armistice of November, 1918.

One essay in *Small Things* but not published in *Woman's Home Companion* was "Beads," published first in *Harper's Monthly.*[9] In this she repeats none of the clichés; instead, she talks of her uncertainties about what victory over Germany would bring. Writing from Paris, she evokes the tension, expectations, and fears of those waiting for war to end. Deland uses the metaphor of stringing colored beads to symbolize the shifting emotions of those waiting for the end—crimson for fury, crystal for tears, black for fear, and gold for trust in God. She shifts in her color

selections just as emotions were shifting in Paris. The essay
was harshly criticized as pro-German because Deland warned
that the Allies needed rebirth as much as Germany. The materialism of civilization had created war, she said, and an Allied victory
would preserve materialism. Her cast of characters in the essay
debates the merits of victory, suggesting that perhaps only destroying civilization could save it to rise again to true spiritual
values. "Beads" is a contrast to the other pieces on the war
because Deland pauses in her wholehearted support of the Allies
to contemplate the effects of war, the killing, the brutalization
of both the victors and the defeated. It is her only thoughtful
look at World War I, probably the precursor of *The Kays.*

A few of her last essays are concerned with communication
with the dead. By the end of the war she had a distinct hope
that survival of the spirit was a reality, and she had had ouija
board experiences that seemed to be caused by her husband
trying to reach her after his death. Although she dismissed most
psychic experiences as coincidence, telepathy, or unconscious
memories, she did come to believe by the 1920s that there
were enough inexplicable stories for her to be confident in the
survival of individual identity.

The Autobiographies

If This Be I, As I Suppose It Be.   Margaret Deland's first
autobiography, *If This Be I, As I Suppose It Be* (1935), focuses
on Maggie Campbell at age six to eight, living at Maple Grove,
Pennsylvania, with her Campbell cousins. The book is written
not as an "I remember" but in the third person, as Margaret
Deland reports the activities of Maggie, one of the many selves
that have been Margaret Deland over the years. The adult Margaret reports events as Maggie remembers them, some clear,
some fuzzy. There are no dates, no chronology. The book is
a series of vignettes, showing Maggie as she plays and experiences the world, which is endlessly fascinating to her.

Deland here, as she had in much of her fiction, evokes the
mid-nineteenth-century life of a child who is growing during
the Civil War, surrounded by restrictions of Victorian propriety
and Puritan morality but involved in the eternal concerns of a

child—dirt, cookies, and imagination. Maggie Campbell in the 1860s plays with her toad, learns her Ten Commandments without understanding them, and struggles to earn the dimes her foster mother will pay her for digging weeds. Maggie's stories in this book are grouped into clusters that illustrate a concept, such as truth, justice, fear, and God, that the child encountered during those years. Thus, Deland recounts that Maggie learns patriotism by waving to departing Union soldiers as they went South to face the Confederates; Maggie, however, supposes that patriotism and war mean "the same thing."[10] She learns propriety when, lacking a handkerchief to wave, she strips off her drawers and waves them until horrified aunts seize her. Her first notion that there might be something unpleasant about war comes when she finds a servant burying the family silver in anticipation of one of Morgan's raids, and she begins to fear that "Mr. Morgan" will steal her hens.

When Maggie encounters the word *justice,* she associates it with punishment and so constructs a gallows on which she manages to hang twelve locusts by their "necks." When she decides to be compassionate, she creates a "hospital" for bugs, forcing reluctant caterpillars into her mustard plasters and pinning them to little beds. The results of Maggie's "justice" and "compassion" are nearly the same, until the caterpillars manage to escape. Deland shows the girl's literal and logical mind trying to copy the adult versions of the new ideas she encounters daily.

Maggie's early idea of God is that of "a fat man with white whiskers" (180). Curious, she asks the childish questions that frustrate adults. "If God can do anything, why doesn't He kill the bad devil?" (183). She notices that God apparently does not answer all prayers. He doesn't make Maggie's hair curly as she prays nor does He shut down Schneider's saloon as the temperance ladies pray. Deland remarks that God gradually ceased to interest Maggie although the religious atmosphere in which she lived continued to provide her with a specific concept of God and religious doctrine.

Throughout *If This Be I,* there are bits and pieces of Maggie's memories that over the years appeared in Margaret Deland's fiction. Maggie's childhood physician is named Dr. King. Grandmother Wade's cook is called Flora, as is the cook in *The Rising Tide.* Maggie makes hollyhock ladies as Mr. Tommy Dove did, and she plays the games that Deland's fictional children played. Maggie's foster father takes responsibility for a debt he doesn't owe as Lloyd Pryor did in *The Awakening of Helena Richie.* The portrait of Maggie's foster mother is a loving picture of a woman who embodies the standards and gentility of an age, the kind of woman Helena Richie learns to be. Margaret Deland comments that years later she realized that her foster mother had infinite love for and patience with her. At the time Maggie was growing up, however, Mrs. Campbell often seemed to be stifling her creative urges, particularly if Maggie was tempted to fib. Primarily, however, Mrs. Campbell taught Maggie honor and duty, and those concepts are the themes in much of her writing. A less stern influence was Grandmother Wade in Pittsburgh. The Episcopalian grandparents lacked the discipline of the Presbyterian parents, and Maggie's early taste of a less restricted life may have planted the seeds for her later rebellion against Calvinism and religious orthodoxy.

The adult Margaret Deland who repeats the child Maggie's memories in this book often says that she is horrified at the curious, blunt, fearless, and savage Maggie. Yet that curiosity and fearlessness later created the writer who probed human passions, attacked human stupidity, and criticized those who shirked their duty.

If This Be I is one of Deland's finest books—an impressionistic and captivating view of the explorations of a child. Coming after the disappointing *Captain Archer's Daughter,* the book reaffirms Deland's ability to create a dynamic personality. The last pages wherein Maggie talks to the earth and then kisses it rank with the most moving Deland ever wrote.

Golden Yesterdays.   Published when Margaret Deland was 84, *Golden Yesterdays* (1941) is the story of her marriage to Lorin Fuller Deland. She begins the book with her teen years, almost bringing *If This Be I* up to date as the teenage Margaret continues to display the curiosity and independence of the child Maggie. At Pelham Priory, the very proper boarding school for young ladies, Margaret is dropped to the bottom of the Role of Honor—for running in the halls. In spite of Mrs. Campbell's attempt to discourage an interest in money, by the time Margaret Deland is thirteen she is thinking of ways to earn her own living. When she is twenty-one, she meets Lorin Deland

and "the two brooks became a River, the two lives one Life."[11] The rest of the book concerns their life together.

The marriage appears to have been an extraordinarily happy one. It is possible that Deland, writing in her eighties, had filtered out any bad memories, but it is more likely that she and Lorin Deland were suited in intellect, temperament, and aesthetic taste to a degree that is relatively rare. The fact that there were no children was disappointing but no doubt contributed to the two becoming full partners in all their activities, and allowing Margaret Deland's writing career to develop. Her memories of her literary career record her husband's encouragement. He gave her the idea for *The Awakening of Helena Richie.* He titled most of her works and acted as one of her most critical editors. She dedicated nearly all her books to him, once calling him her "patient, ruthless, inspiring critic."[12]

Golden Yesterdays, while more chronological than *If This Be I,* does not record events and dates in a strictly organized fashion. Deland is moving through her memories of her marriage and the active life she and Lorin Deland shared in Boston. She moves back and forth in time, explaining, for instance, her deep involvement in helping unwed mothers, and then going back to catch up on other events. Her memories provide a fascinating look at Boston in the last twenty years of the nineteenth century. The two aggressive and eager-to-be-involved young people gradually join Boston's intellectual and business circles. Lorin Deland took an interest in government, charity, the theater, sports, and nearly everything else, and Margaret kept pace with him.

The book is essentially the record of the first twenty years of the Deland marriage, from 1880 to 1900. The story for the years 1900 to 1917 is highly compressed, covered in only fifty pages. The book ends in 1917 with Lorin Deland's death, which Margaret called "the end of my world" (350). She lived another twenty-seven years, continuing to publish and lecture, but she felt her life was "darkened" by his absence.

Golden Yesterdays is a storehouse of bits of firsthand knowledge of the greats of the nineteenth century—Julia Ward Howe, Dr. Edward Everett Hale, President Theodore Roosevelt, Rudyard Kipling. Deland knew them all, and her memories provide a glimpse of the human being behind the public image. She tells

the charming story of how Dr. Hale dropped in to get an address
for a party at which he was expected and spent the afternoon
with her instead, drinking sherry and talking.

The Deland friendship with the great Boston minister Phillips
Brooks was very important, particularly because, when they met
him, the Delands were young and poor and unimportant. The
Phillips Brooks in *Golden Yesterdays* is a warm, generous man,
never too busy to respond to those who need him, even young
couples who don't belong to his church. He and Lorin Deland
collaborated on a series of lectures for the residents of Boston's
skid row area. Margaret Deland solicited his advice on her poetry, on her first novel, on her loss of faith, and on her many
charity projects. The shocked reactions of Boston residents to
the news of Brooks's unexpected death show how revered the
Episcopalian bishop was. Lorin Deland arranged for a death
mask, knowing that there would be statues and busts in honor
of the religious leader. The memory of Brooks remained important to Margaret Deland throughout her life. Her last published
essay was a portrait of Phillips Brooks that she was writing
for *Golden Yesterdays*. [13]

Mingled with these memories are the clues to the sources
of some of her work. Her foster father's reaction to his wife's
death became the basis of the short story "The Third Volume."
The unwed mothers who lived in her house became her fictional
fallen women. Traces of Dr. Lavendar appear in the picture
of Phillips Brooks. Eleanor in *The Vehement Flame* experiences
some of Deland's first struggles with housekeeping. Margaret
Deland's description of the death of Lorin Deland's father is
particularly dramatic and moving; it was, she wrote, "when the
significance of Love and Death first struck me" (93). She says
that she learned then that, because love and death both exist,
human beings must experience grief—a concept that became
the basis for her second novel, *Sidney*.

Golden Yesterdays marked the end of Margaret Deland's fifty-
six-year writing career. The core of her talent had always been
the ability to delineate the individual. Her last work showed
that ability undiminished as she described with her sure touch
those whom she had loved most.

Chapter Seven

The Reputation and the Talent

Margaret Deland began her career writing a novel of religious controversy. The major women novelists in America up to then had been primarily writers of the domestic romance. Augusta Evans Wilson, Mary Jane Holmes, Elizabeth Stuart Phelps, and E. D. E. N. Southworth all wrote novels wherein virginal young women endured great hardship but at last won the love of handsome, gallant, and (usually) very rich men. Other women writers, such as Rose Terry Cooke, Mary Murfree, and Sarah Orne Jewett wrote stories of local color. Deland fit neither group very well. However, by the 1890s, a new generation of women writers emerged. Edith Wharton, Ellen Glasgow, and Gertrude Atherton wrote about the serious concerns of women and appealed to a new audience of women. Deland's career flowered during a time when women writers and the issues they dealt with were taken more seriously than they had been before. Once having established her audience, Deland continued to write and sell through the decades of change. By the end of her career she was regarded as the beloved representative of a past era.

Critical Response

Margaret Deland's first novel created such shock and, in some quarters, outrage that critics reviewed her work seriously from the beginning. The *Church Quarterly Review* said that *John Ward, Preacher* showed "considerable creative ability" in character and setting, but criticized the book for implying that there was no alternative to rejecting the Bible.[1] In general, the clergy disliked Deland's attack on orthodoxy. One minister said that the novel lacked "genius," but because it was widely read he felt that he had to discuss it.[2] More secular criticism in *Life* magazine (May 3, 1888) called the story "provokingly narrow." The controversy helped establish Deland as a serious writer, and her next novels, although rather unsuccessful in sales, got careful consideration from contemporary critics. Most reviews were mixed. Deland's minor characters were singled out for praise while her major themes were attacked. *Sidney* was criticized for being "destitute of local color," the reviewer complaining that it was English in tone.[3] Deland was called an artist of "true perceptions" in a review which also said she had "no defined and positive doctrine to enunciate."[4]

The world of Old Chester earned for Deland almost universal praise from reviewers. She began to be the subject of articles reviewing her work as a whole. Critics sometimes connected her specifically with women's issues and analyzed her as a "woman writer"; one reviewer praised her "rare and large-hearted womanliness which sympathizes with erring women."[5] She was included in *The Women Who Make Our Novels,* where her books were called "biographies" because of the reality of the characters. "She is the ideal biographer. . . . taking infinite pains and exhibiting an infinite comprehension of and sympathy with simple and memorable lives."[6]

After the publication of *The Awakening of Helena Richie* the editor and critic Mark De Wolfe Howe said Margaret Deland had three talents peculiarly her own—a knowledge of the mind of a child, a familiarity with the small town, and an understanding of the relations of men and women.[7] Some reviewers felt that Deland's stress on ethical questions kept her out of the ranks of domestic novelists and "in the same class . . . as Mrs. Gaskell and Jane Austen."[8] Fred Lewis Pattee said her aim was to "expose the human soul . . . to show it its limitations and its dangers, that the soul may be purged. . . ." He also described her talent as both masculine and feminine. "To feminine tenderness and insight she added a depth of view and an analysis that is masculine."[9] Pattee and others called *The Awakening of Helena Richie* and *The Iron Woman* Deland's finest creations. Henry Mills Alden, the editor of *Harper's Monthly,* wrote that Deland was in the long line of successful women novelists following Fanny Burney and had become the "exemplar" of writers of realistic fiction.[10] The praise for both *The Iron Woman* and *The Awakening of Helena Richie* was nearly universal, although one critic refused to accept Helena as such a "pagan,"[11] and another was disappointed in its "skimming the laughing surfaces of life."[12]

Deland's Old Chester drew comparisons with other literary creations. Thomas Hardy's Wessex, Elizabeth Gaskell's Cranford, and Arnold Bennett's Five Towns were mentioned as comparable to Old Chester. Most often Deland was compared to Jane Austen: "In her delineations of everyday characters, in her keen and humorous insight, Mrs. Deland is not excelled by Jane Austen herself."[13]

Deland and Austen do share a common concentration on character over plot. The ironic and objective view of people and human foibles came through the objective narration both Austen and Deland employed. The reader is never completely enveloped in the consciousness of the main character but is always sufficiently distant so as to see both Fred Payton's youthful callousness and Emma Woodhouse's smug self-satisfaction. Realistic detail in setting and character also connects Austen and Deland. The activities of daily life, the importance of small things, the norms of the middle class were the foundations for Deland's work as they had been for Austen's.

World War I brought changes in literature, public taste, and critical attitudes. Deland's later works still sold to the audience she had built up over the years, but critics tended to put her in the past, a representative of a time now gone. A review of *The Vehement Flame* said she was of the "pre-Dreiserian era and writes about life as it ought to be."[14] A *New York Times* reviewer liked *The Kays* but called it "dated." Deland's gentle memories of the past did not excite the critical imagination now intrigued by such writers as Ernest Hemingway, John Steinbeck, and William Faulkner.

Although she had earlier been criticized for lacking local color, she now began to be called a local colorist. Carl Van Doren slashed at the endings of her novels—"soft with a sentimentalism swathed in folds of piety." Deland, he said, was good only when she concentrated on small detail, when she adhered to "the parochial cult of local color."[15] Praise came most for her short stories, and short stories from women almost inevitably were regarded as local color. Old Chester, however, was not especially reflective of a particular locality. Critics who were determined to place Deland with local colorists handled this difficulty by including Old Chester with the New England villages of Mary Wilkins Freeman and Sarah Orne Jewett. Fred Lewis Pattee admitted that Old Chester reflected a universal type but added that "It might be New England."[16] Ima Herron discussed Deland's work under "New England Village in a New Light," saying "Such writers as Mrs. Deland and her New England contemporaries have delineated variously a type of small town life now remote . . . the old-fashioned New England village. . . ."[17]

Other critics, however, described her as a writer who dealt with moral and theological problems. She was recognized as a realist, a follower of William Dean Howells, her material not local but ethical and universal. Arthur Hobson Quinn called her a "classic realist" who retained "an objective attitude toward the social, ethical and religious problems."[18] The interest in her, however, was becoming largely historical; she came from and wrote about another era. After her death she ceased to be mentioned in literary discussions of important writers and faded from all but the most comprehensive literary dictionaries.

The developing interest in popular literature in the 1960s brought Margaret Deland back to the attention of critics. The New Criticism of the 1940s and 1950s, concentrating on textual analysis, had shut Deland out. Today the rising interest in popular culture as reflecting the social and intellectual history of a period has led to a partial rediscovery of Margaret Deland. Moreover, the strong interest in women writers of the past who were successful and, therefore, influential has also contributed to reviving Deland's name. Barbara Welter, in her *Dimity Convictions,* includes Deland in a discussion of women novelists of religious controversy who rejected the traditional religious dogma and searched for a new, more moderate faith. Welter believes that Deland and other women such as Augusta Evans Wilson and Elizabeth Stuart Phelps are absent from histories of American thought because they were popular women writers; however, these women, Welter says, filled an important role as popular theologians, showing a Christianity that could flourish in the midst of change, a Christianity that was more merciful than the traditional creeds.

In a recent study of women's fiction in America, *Who Is in the House?,* Sally McNall discusses what she regards as the struggle to recognize the self in popular novels by women. She cites Deland as creating mothers that neglect or stifle their children (*The Promises of Alice, The Iron Woman*) as well as women who must stifle their own sexuality (Elizabeth in *The Iron Woman,* Helena in *The Awakening of Helena Richie*).

Deland has recently been categorized as modern and innovative for her time. Comparing her with Gertrude Atherton, Herbert Smith describes Deland as "thoroughly modern about sex as Atherton is old-fashioned."[19] Smith feels that *John Ward, Preacher* has "aged extremely well, chiefly because of the balanced portraits of . . . two opposed orthodoxies" (157). It is that balance that makes her modern. "In her work as a whole, nothing is sacred or profane" (162).

Other recent critics have sometimes contrasted her novels specifically with novels by her contemporaries, speculating about influences. *John Ward, Preacher* is suggested as being influential in Harold Frederic's *The Damnation of Theron Ware* (1896).[20] The dangers of the zealot in Frederic's novel parallel those in Deland's work as the elders eject unbelievers from the church.

Robert McIlvaine speculates that *The Awakening of Helena Richie* was a direct response to Kate Chopin's novel, *The Awakening.*[21] He cites the similarity of titles and the fact that Deland's book was called simply *The Awakening* during her writing of it as indications that Deland meant to refute Chopin's story of a woman who flouts convention. In fact, it is unlikely that Deland was concerned with refuting Chopin's novel if she even knew of its existence. She reports in *Golden Yesterdays* how difficult it was to write her book and how she had to search for a theme and plot. Lorin Deland finally produced a twenty-page outline to get her started, and he later titled the book. Deland herself sometimes used the shortened title *The Awakening* to refer to her book, and years later, in 1920, critic Blanche Williams still referred to the book by its shortened title. Deland never mentions "responding" to any writer's work throughout her long career. Her belief in the categorical imperative and, therefore, her natural contrast with Chopin's theme dated back to *Philip and His Wife* in 1894, and the theme of accepting individual responsibility was a constant in her fiction. What such speculation shows is that Deland again has a place in the critical awareness of past literature. And, unlike some popular writers who are remembered chiefly for one wildly successful book, Margaret Deland is important to the study of popular literature because of her work's continuing reflection of her times and attitudes. Her major themes dealing with women, with individual duty, with moderation and intellect provide those who study popular literature with various windows to her society.

Women's Concerns

Margaret Deland was not a "women's writer" as others were who wrote the popular domestic-sentimental novels. She was a writer who examined problems—primarily those of human relations and human responsibility. As a woman, however, she found the concerns of women most interesting to her, and her focus tended toward women and their place, their problems, their responsibilities.

She saw women's independence as something that would enhance society and solve many of the concerns of women. Her fear was that the desire for change and the impatience for independence would bring down what she felt was the foundation of society—the family. She urged selective criticism of society; nothing was all bad or all good. Women must use their minds; if they did, Deland believed, many of the problems and inequities surrounding women could be eradicated.

Although she often wrote about weak or oppressive men, she did not heap the blame for women's problems on men. Her fictional women were at fault for supporting or encouraging their men in their weaknesses. Miss Maria refuses to admit her nephew's incompetence with money. She literally gives him everything and says nothing critical when he loses it all. In "The Thief" Annie is blind to her husband's shallowness and so encourages his inability to take action. Blair Maitland in *The Iron Woman* has been pampered by his mother and allowed to grow up without any sense of responsibility or training in making a living. The men in Deland's fiction who are dictatorial and oppressive usually lose their power when women make intellectual decisions and defy them. Helen refuses to give in to John Ward's demand that she accept his religious beliefs. Sidney has accepted her father's dictates but throws them off when she allows herself to explore her own consciousness. Helena is able to throw off

Lloyd Pryor's dominance when she begins to realize her responsibilities. The Halsey sisters defy the power of their tyrannical father and destroy his will ("The Harvest of Fear"). Essentially, Margaret Deland did not blame men for the problems of women but saw women's difficulties as resulting from the absence of intellectual independence and a lack of practical knowledge of the world.

Her work with unwed mothers had revealed to her the ignorance most girls had about sexual matters. She became a strong advocate for sex education, writing much more directly about such matters than most of her contemporaries. She urged parents to accept the responsibility of teaching youngsters about sex. Her long sympathy toward the struggle of the unwed mother was mirrored in the portrait of Katy McGrath, who sacrifices to give her daughter an education and advantages ("The Eliots' Katy"). Deland felt sure that if women had adequate sexual knowledge they could avoid Katy's problems and also the kind of problem represented by the severely retarded Mortimore, the result of his father's syphilitic infection (*The Rising Tide*). In that novel Fred shocks others by frankly blaming Mortimore's existence on the ignorance of her mother; if women were not kept ignorant of the consequences of sexual dissipation, she says, they would be in a position to pressure men to give up their excesses. It was the idea that innocence equaled ignorance that perpetuated such tragedies. Fred lobbies for legislation to require health certificates before marriage and says that women must refuse to accept sexual vice as "natural" for men. In addition, she insists that sex education would result in more birth control and the oppressive burden of too many children would be lifted from women. *The Rising Tide* is Margaret Deland's most explicit treatment of the need for sex education for women. Many of her stories and articles, however, made the same point.

Because Deland believed primarily in intelligence as the key to solving societal problems, she did not believe that getting the vote would appreciably increase women's wages or improve working conditions. She had, however, a strong interest in the financial problems of women in a society that gave them few choices in finding ways to earn their bread. Many of her short stories pointed out the helplessness of women who must earn their own way and have no means to do so. The sick desperation

of women losing the only position available to them is the theme
of *Partners*. The problem of earning a living after her nephew
loses her small income is "ghastly" to elderly Miss Maria. All
the women are willing to work and want to be independent,
but society gives them no training and no opportunity to be
economically free. Moreover, those who struggle to earn a living
are pitied or even disapproved of by others. Added to the struggle then is the emotional ordeal of being the object of the
pity and gossip of one's neighbors. Although Deland frequently
rescued her women with marriage (the only really viable solution in Old Chester), she vividly illustrated the need for economic opportunity—one of the pressing problems of women.

Changes were needed, and the "new woman" at the end of
the nineteenth century was part of the change. Deland supported
change as long as it did not mean an abdication of individual
responsibility. She believed that too intense a concentration on
individualism could cause a woman to abandon her duty, and
she did not want the family to suffer, thinking as her contemporaries did that the woman was the force that held the family
together. The ideal woman would combine individualism and
responsibility and be guided by her intellect.

Margaret Deland's fiction contains many vivid portraits of
intellectually acute women. Her "girls," such as Alicia Drayton
(*Philip and His Wife*), Alice Alden (*The Promises of Alice*), and
Lois Howe (*John Ward, Preacher*), tend to be standard romantic
heroines, timid and susceptible to the pressure and manipulations of others. But Deland's "women," such as Cecil Shore
(*Philip and His Wife*), Agnes Kay (*The Kays*), and Sarah Maitland
(*The Iron Woman*), are complex and varied personalities. They
are not especially young. Fred Payton in *The Rising Tide* is one
of the youngest at twenty-five. The women, moreover, are not
timid or helpless as romantic heroines often are, but are confident and trust themselves and their judgment.

Helena Richie in *The Iron Woman* most nearly embodies what
Margaret Deland believed was an ideal woman. Helena is a
woman of intellect, strength, and independent moral judgment.
She is not swayed by momentary passions although she may
sympathize with them. She sees her responsibility and fulfills
it. At the same time, she retains what Deland felt was a crucial
feminine charm, precluding the strident personality that Deland

saw in many feminists and portrayed in Fred Payton. Fred has a vigorous independence and a dynamic intellect, but she ignores personal responsibility to work on her causes. And her often shocking comments and actions hurt others. In the end, when Fred learns humility, she is closer to Deland's ideal, since her intellect is undiminished but she has lost her conceit and accepted her responsibilities.

It is intellect that distinguishes Deland's women. From the cool calculating mind of Cecil Shore to the grimly rigid Agnes Kay, the major women characters analyze their situations, their relationships, and make decisions on the basis of reasoned judgment. Even when the woman's motivating force is love, as when Rose Knight refuses to release her fiancé from the engagement ("How *COULD* She!"), the woman bases her actions on intellectual assessment of the situation.

In Deland's fiction problems are a result of a woman's failure to integrate intellect with what Deland believed was a natural feminine instinct to support the family. Sarah Maitland can run an iron works, but she has no idea how to raise her children.

Margaret Deland's realistic portrayal of society led her into attacking many of the clichés that were attached to women. Her women in financial difficulty illustrated the inadequacy of the notion that women did not need education. All women did not have men to support them, and Deland showed the need for an opportunity to earn a living with dignity.

The common idea that for a woman any marriage was better than none was refuted in her pictures of failed marriages. Several women show that one can live quite contentedly without marrying. Clara Hale is too content to ever consider marrying her long-time suitor ("Miss Clara's Perseus"), and Lydia Sampson desperately manipulates her fiancé into jilting her so she can continue her single life ("The Grasshopper and the Ant"). The women in Deland's fiction may wish for a home and family, but, like Rose Knight, they will not settle for what they know would be less than a successful match. Nina Morgan refuses to marry the man she loves in *The Hands of Esau* because he is too weak to face her with the truth. Edith Houghton in *The Vehement Flame,* on the other hand, stands by Maurice because he is strong enough to accept his responsibilities.

The best marriages in Deland's work are unions of two people of equal and compatible intellect who accept and support each other. Fred Payton and Arthur Weston in *The Rising Tide* represent such a couple, as do Edith Houghton and Maurice Curtis in *The Vehement Flame.* In both cases the couples have already been through adversity and have accepted each other's mistakes. Other satisfactory unions involve people of good will who have a genuine interest in helping each other. Often those unions are the result of a man coming to the rescue of a financially pressed woman ("Miss Clara's Perseus," "House of Rimmon," "Miss Maria," "The Unexpectedness of Mr. Horace Shields").

Deland's fiction shows clearly that romantic love is poor grounds for marriage. Matches made on that basis end in bitter, loveless marriages in which the two people have no common interests or intellectual agreement. Sexual attraction and romantic delusion are strong but temporary, as the couples in *Captain Archer's Daughter, Philip and His Wife,* and *The Kays* discover. True love in Deland's fiction grows slowly over a long period of time (David and Elizabeth in *The Iron Woman,* Cap and Bess in *Captain Archer's Daughter,* Lois and Gifford in *John Ward, Preacher*).

Deland treated a few of the traditional images of women with a humor designed to demolish those images as serious reflections of women's state. The long tradition that the jilted woman must take to her bed gets humorous treatment in "The Promises of Dorothea" when Mary Ferris stays in bed for thirty years. When Mary finally gets up, her sister Clara is crushed that the romantic image is ended. Another cliché Deland dismissed was that all women had a natural inclination for domestic duties. Her major women characters often do not demonstrate either successful motherhood or domestic talents. Eleanor in *The Vehement Flame* is totally helpless in the kitchen. Mattie Archer does not want her child and does not like him after she has him (*Captain Archer's Daughter*). Mrs. King's sister Lucy can't sew, cook, or keep house, and she has no desire to learn ("The Unexpectedness of Mr. Horace Shields").

Perhaps most vigorously Deland attacked the helpless, mindless woman who lives as a parasite on her husband and on society. *The Vehement Flame* demolished the idea that a beautiful woman who has never used her mind could be interesting. "Amelia" is about a vague, empty woman who can never quite understand her husband or children. Disdain is heaped on the men who marry these women. Deland remarks caustically that a man never married a woman because she was sensible, and most men prefer fools. The man who marries a fool "wants to have her for his wife—to do as he wishes, to think as he thinks, to echo his opinions, and to admire his conduct."[22] She had little hope of changing men who, she said, were essentially polygamous at heart. Change would come from women. As long as women remained foolish and helpless, they would lack independence. For Deland, woman's independence lay in her mind; she had only to use it.

Moderation

For Margaret Deland, one of the great evils of the world was fanaticism. She began her writing career with the portrait of the religious fanaticism of Presbyterian John Ward and over the years continued to examine the devastating effect fanatics have on themselves and on those around them. The dangers she saw came from the fanatic's need to control others, to make them join in the devotion to a cause.

The religious fanatic, such as John Ward, usually warps the lives of those he professes to love the most. John Ward destroys his marriage when Helen refuses to accept his view of salvation. Athalia Hall also destroys her marriage (*The Way to Peace*). Mrs. Alden extracts a promise of missionary work from her daughter Alice, who has no desire to leave her home (*The Promises of Alice*). Agnes Kay's extremism encompasses both her religion and her social conscience. Her son becomes isolated from society as she imposes her dogmatic ideas on him. The fanatical rejection of religion can be equally destructive, as Sidney's father, Major Lee, proves when he tries to keep her from love and marriage. Deland's own liberal beliefs were antagonistic to any extremism in the name of religion. She felt that the religious fanatic destroyed the innocent—a direct contradiction of the purpose of religious faith. Her stories reveal the frustration and tension of those who have to deal with the fanatic's demands.

Another type of fanaticism that Margaret Deland abhorred was that devotion to an ideal that had no basis in practicality. Aunt Adelaide in *The Rising Tide* sacrifices her life to caring for a severely retarded brother, turning down several offers of marriage. Self-sacrifice for no useful purpose was "spiritual dissipation" in Deland's view: devotion to duty must be practical. Dr. Lavendar often counsels his parishioners to do the practical thing rather than follow the ideal that will not serve any useful purpose. In "The Law, Or the Gospel" Sara Wharton finds that she has squandered her money and her energy trying to reform Nellie Sherman, who doesn't want to reform. Sara has no help left to give to those who truly want it. In Deland's world the ideal must always have a practical basis. One of the worst faults of any extremist is a lack of common sense.

Deland's opposition to some of the feminist positions was rooted in what she saw as the extremism in the movement. Fred Payton mouths many of the feminist clichés—with no regard for the sensibilities of her listeners. Worse, however, in Deland's view was the danger that the extremists would perpetrate greater evils than the ones they sought to eradicate. When feminists swore to close houses of prostitution, Deland knew from her charity work that the women would move to the streets and probably make a better living. She also predicted an increase in drunkenness if the saloons were closed. She believed that spirituality could not be legislated. Moreover, the freedom to choose goodness was what made people strong. If they lacked the freedom to choose, they lacked independence. Deland feared that the feminist cry to independence would curtail the independence of others.

Most important to true independence, she felt, was the categorical imperative—the individual is not free to do what he wants if that same action, done by everyone, would destroy society. To make that choice to support society, people needed to be free to use their minds, to assess the risks in a situation, to choose responsibility over selfishness. The fanatic in any cause seeks to remove that freedom of choice, and throughout Margaret Deland's long career she argued against all extreme positions. Moderation was the key. "Do not haste. Do not hold back," she once wrote.[23]

The Talent

Margaret Deland belongs to the late nineteenth-century American realistic movement led by such writers as William

Dean Howells and emphasizing the truthful treatment of detail and character. Middle-class society, the common and daily life, the ethical issues that touch everyone—these concern the realist and certainly concerned Margaret Deland.

Although some stories, such as "A Black Drop," touched the lower classes, most of Deland's work focused on the middle class. Her Old Chester society contained teachers, lawyers, businessmen, and ministers. Those in financial straits, such as Miss Maria Welwood, were of the background that qualified them for society as long as they maintained the gentility of manners their station required. Deland's portraits of the people who made up her world were those of the realist who sees the foolish and the wise, the good and the bad, the predictable and the inconsistent in human behavior. Plot was simple; she concentrated on the interactions of her characters and their struggles with what she regarded as serious ethical questions of independent thought and duty. Her realism was coupled with optimism because she believed that writers who showed only the evils that existed were ignoring some of the truth of life. She refused to show a world without love.

Margaret Deland's special talent was characterization. Her insight into the mind of a child in such works as *The Story of a Child, The Iron Woman,* and *The Kays* makes her the equal of Mark Twain in capturing the essence of childhood. Deland's children were not as adventurous as Tom Sawyer or Huck Finn, but their minds were as active, their dreams as large, and her depiction of their frustrations, trials, and triumphs was as vivid and true as Twain's stories about children. In her treatment of children Margaret Deland was markedly different from the other popular writers who usually created teary and tragic little orphans to excite the reader's sympathy and churn up events in the melodramatic plots. Deland's children exercised independent minds. Limited by age and circumstance, they fantasized their adventures. Their restrictions and their rebellions reflect their society and its values; their fantasies show that the mind cannot be restricted.

Deland's special talent in characterization also proved itself in her women. Sarah Maitland, Helen Ward, Katy McGrath, and Mattie Archer illustrate psychological and social variety. Even minor characters, such as the elderly women, show De-

land's insight into the psychological variety in character. Mrs.
Paul harbors resentment for twenty-five years (*Sidney*); Lydia
Sampson, an eccentric spinster, turns into a fiercely protective
mother ("An Old Chester Secret"); fluttery, idle Mrs. Newboldt
gives her niece shrewd advice on holding her marriage together
(*The Vehement Flame*).

Although she has been called a representative of local color,
Margaret Deland was never a writer of local color. The primary
concern of such a writer—the speech, dress, mannerisms, and
customs peculiar to a particular region—is not present in Deland's writings. She was not concerned with regional peculari-
ties: her interest was universal human nature, the moral base
of civilization. Her characters could have lived in any area of
the United States or even in England. Old Chester lacked any
regional distinction; it was of a time and society rather than
of a place. In fact, when Deland set some stories in other places
(*The Promises of Alice, Captain Archer's Daughter*), there was no
major difference between those villages and Old Chester.

Margaret Deland expressed the spirit of her time, the feelings
unique to her society. Her work is a mirror of the relationships,
the problems, the moral crises of an age. She supported the
independence of women as long as they accepted individual
responsibility. She probed the issues that she felt were crucial
to true independence for women: financial opportunity, sex education, and freedom to exercise judgment. Her women struggled
with the concerns of all intelligent women of their time; they
achieved some successes without destroying their society; the
best of them kept their intellectual independence. They were
models of women who could think, who could fight the worst
inequities, who could fulfill responsibility, and yet who could
hold society together.

Most important, Margaret Deland struck a balance that was
acceptable to her readers. She raised the serious questions concerning women, but she did not advocate destroying the society
that created these questions. She relied on the intelligence of
individuals both to maintain and to change the social structure.
Her solutions to problems did not often break new ground.
Frequently, her happy endings had to retreat to the traditional—
women rescued by marriage. Her examination of the issues
raised questions, but her happy endings assured readers that

the issues could be resolved. Her popularity indicates that readers felt comfortable with the balance she maintained between criticism and support for society.

It may be, however, that Margaret Deland was more radical than she knew herself. Having once raised the issues, she probed them mercilessly. *The Vehement Flame* is a fierce attack on the useless woman. The need for sex education is glaringly obvious in *The Rising Tide*. Even though she opposed divorce, Deland's fictional marriages were often strong cases for the ending of a marriage. She introduced a great many readers to the severity of the problems women faced, and she articulated the importance of those problems. Perhaps her readers looked beyond her moderate solutions and, in fact, moved to the more radical answers. The changes that took place during Deland's writing years may have sprung in part from some of the readers who looked at her picture of the world and decided that moderation was not enough.

If popularity is any guide, Margaret Deland offered the moderate position readers could be comfortable with. But she also took controversial positions, advocating significant change in her society. Her work remains for us one of the clearest reflections of woman's place and woman's possibilities in her time.

Notes and References

Chapter One

1. *Golden Yesterdays* (New York, 1941), p. 1; hereafter cited in the text as *GY* followed by page number.
2. *If This Be I, As I Suppose It Be* (New York, 1935), p. 101; hereafter cited in the text as *ITBI* followed by page number.
3. Joe Mitchell Chapple, "Margaret Deland," *National Magazine* (Boston) 9 (March, 1899):524.
4. Albert Frederick Wilson, "Can Children Be Taught to Write?" *Good Housekeeping* 61 (July, 1915).47.
5. "I Didn't Know—," *Ladies' Home Journal* 24 (March, 1907):9.
6. *The Story of Delia* (Boston, [1920?]), p. 7.
7. *Critic,* March 4, 1893, p. 126.
8. *Chap-Book* 7 (June 1, 1897):65.
9. *Outlook,* December 17, 1898, p. 972.
10. *Harper's Weekly,* November 14, 1903, p. 1839.
11. "Individualism and Social Responsibility," *Independent,* May 23, 1901, p. 1174.
12. "The Change in the Feminine Ideal," *Atlantic Monthly* 105 (March, 1910):290.
13. Ibid., p. 298.
14. "The Third Way in Woman Suffrage," *Ladies' Home Journal* 30 (January, 1913):11.
15. "Woman in the Market Place," *Independent,* May 22, 1916, pp. 288.
16. *Harper's Weekly,* August 4, 1906, p. 1110.
17. *Dial* 51 (December 1, 1911):473.
18. "Things We Thought Were Big," *Small Things* (New York, 1919), p. 182.
19. "The Doors of Silence: A Discussion of the Possibilities of Communication with Those Who Have Died," *Woman's Home Companion* 46 (November, 1919):7.
20. Deland to Edward Sandford Martin, July 21, 1922, Edward Sandford Martin Papers, Houghton Library, Harvard University, Cambridge, Mass.
21. "A Peak in Darien," in *The Case For And Against Psychial*

Belief, ed. Carl Murchison (Worcester, Mass.: Clark University Press, 1927), p. 145.

22. *Saturday Review of Literature,* February 5, 1927, p. 561.

23. *Time,* January 22, 1945, p. 68.

24. "The Truth of the Novel," *Independent,* April 6, 1899, p. 952.

Chapter Two

1. *John Ward, Preacher* (1888; reprint, Ridgewood, N.J., 1967), p. 40. Page numbers in parentheses in the text refer to this edition.

2. *Life,* May 3, 1888, p. 250.

3. *Sidney* (Boston, 1890), p. 54. Page numbers in parentheses refer to this edition.

4. *Life,* December 11, 1890, p. 336.

5. *Philip and His Wife* (Boston, 1894), p. 82. Page numbers in parentheses refer to this edition.

Chapter Three

1. "Counting the Cost," *Wisdom of Fools* (Boston, 1897), p. 189.

2. "The Apotheosis of the Reverend Mr. Spangler," *Dr. Lavendar's People* (New York, 1903), p. 4. Page numbers in parentheses refer to this edition.

3. "The Third Volume," *Around Old Chester* (New York, 1915), p. 267. Page numbers in parentheses refer to this edition.

4. "The Promises of Dorothea," *Old Chester Tales* (New York, 1898), p. 9.

5. "A Fourth-Class Appointment," *Mr. Tommy Dove and Other Stories* (Boston, 1893), p. 280.

6. "Miss Maria," *Old Chester Tales* (New York, 1898), p. 117. Page numbers in parentheses refer to this edition.

7. *The Story of a Child* (Boston, 1892), p. 67. Page numbers in parentheses refer to this edition.

8. "The Eliots' Katy," *New Friends in Old Chester* (New York, 1924), p. 31. Page numbers in parentheses refer to this edition.

Chapter Four

1. *The Awakening of Helena Richie* (New York, 1906), p. 276. Page numbers in parentheses refer to this edition.

2. *The Iron Woman* (New York, 1911), pp. 31–32. Page numbers in parentheses refer to this edition.

3. "The Truth of the Novel," *Independent,* April 6, 1899, p. 952.

4. *The Rising Tide* (New York, 1916), p. 66. Page numbers in parentheses refer to this edition.
5. "The Passing of Dora," *Harper's Bazar* 36 (August, 1902): 689–92.
6. "Woman in the Market Place," *Independent,* May 22, 1916, p. 288.

Chapter Five

1. *The Vehement Flame* (New York, 1922), p. 71. Page numbers in parentheses refer to this edition.
2. *The Kays* (New York, 1926), p. 4. Page numbers in parentheses refer to this edition.
3. *Captain Archer's Daughter* (New York, 1932), p. 19. Page numbers in parentheses refer to this edition.

Chapter Six

1. "Polly," in *The Old Garden and Other Verses* (Boston, 1892), p. 113.
2. *Florida Days* (Boston, 1889), p. 181.
3. "Jonquils," *Good Housekeeping* 39 (August, 1904):162–66.
4. "The Shelf," *Harper's Bazar* 36 (April, 1902):361.
5. "When I Was Your Age," *Good Housekeeping* 57 (December, 1913):757.
6. "The Ethics of the Novel," *Independent,* April 13, 1899, p. 1008.
7. "Aunts," *Harper's Bazar* 37 (April, 1903):369–72.
8. "A Deep-Seated Trouble," *Good Housekeeping* 49 (February, 1905):159.
9. "Beads," *Harper's Monthly* 137 (July, 1918):169–77.
10. *If This Be I, As I Suppose It Be* (New York, 1935), p. 29; hereafter page numbers in parentheses refer to this edition.
11. *Golden Yesterdays* (New York, 1941), p. 79; hereafter page numbers in parentheses refer to this edition.
12. *The Iron Woman,* dedication.
13. "Phillips Brooks," *Atlantic Monthly* 166 (July, 1940):29–37.

Chapter Seven

1. *Church Quarterly Review* 29 (January, 1890):346.
2. D. MacMillan, "Recent Religious Novels and the Moral Theory of Another Life," *Scots Magazine* 6 (October, 1890):325.
3. *Critic,* November 22, 1890, p. 256.

4. *Dial* 11 (December, 1890):240.

5. Joe Mitchell Chapple, "Margaret Deland," *National Magazine* (Boston) 9 (March, 1899):526.

6. Grant M. Overton, *The Women Who Make Our Novels* (New York, 1918), pp. 85–86.

7. M. A. De Wolfe Howe, "Margaret Deland: A Study in Influences," *Outlook,* November 24, 1906, p. 731.

8. Mary K. Ford, "Some Representative American Story Tellers. IV.—Margaret Deland," *Bookman* 25 (July, 1907):511.

9. Fred Lewis Pattee, *A History of American Literature Since 1870* (New York, 1917), pp. 395–96.

10. Henry Mills Alden, "The Author of 'The Iron Woman,'" *Outlook,* November 11, 1911, p. 631.

11. *Putnam's Monthly and The New Critic* 1 (October, 1906):109.

12. *North American Review,* September 21, 1906, p. 549.

13. *New York Times Book Review,* July 14, 1906, p. 446.

14. *Dial* 74 (January, 1923):103.

15. Carl Van Doren, *Contemporary American Novelists 1900–1920* (New York, 1931), pp. 22–23.

16. Pattee, *American Literature,* p. 396.

17. Ima Herron, *The Small Town in American Literature* (Durham, N.C., 1939), p. 98.

18. Arthur Hobson Quinn, *American Fiction: An Historical and Critical Survey* (New York, 1936), pp. 468–69.

19. Herbert F. Smith, *The Popular American Novel 1865–1920* (Boston, 1980), p. 149; subsequent page references in this paragraph refer to this work.

20. J. R. K. Kantor, *"The Damnation of Theron Ware* and *John Ward, Preacher,"* *Serif* 3 (March, 1966):16–21.

21. Robert McIlvaine, "Two Awakenings: Edna Pontellier and Helena Richie," *Regionalism and the Female Imagination* 4, no. 3 (1979):44–48.

22. "The Promises of Dorothea," *Old Chester Tales,* p. 25.

23. "The Change in the Feminine Ideal," *Atlantic Monthly* 105 (March, 1910):302.

Selected Bibliography

PRIMARY SOURCES

1. Novels and Novelettes

The Awakening of Helena Richie. New York: Harper & Brothers, 1906. Reprint. Upper Saddle River, N.J.: Literature House, 1969. First published in *Harper's Monthly*, January–July, 1906.

Captain Archer's Daughter. New York: Harper & Brothers, 1932. First published in *Woman's Home Companion*, August, 1931–January, 1932.

An Encore. New York: Harper & Brothers, 1907. First published in *Harper's Monthly*, December, 1904.

Good For the Soul. New York: Harper & Brothers, 1899. First published in *Harper's Monthly*, May, 1898.

The Hands of Esau. New York: Harper & Brothers, 1914. First published in *Woman's Home Companion*, November, 1913–January, 1914.

The Iron Woman. New York: Harper & Brothers, 1911. First published in *Harper's Monthly*, November, 1910–October, 1911.

John Ward, Preacher. Boston: Houghton, Mifflin, 1888. Reprint. Ridgewood, N.J.: Gregg Press, 1967.

The Kays. New York: Harper & Brothers, 1926. First published in *Woman's Home Companion*, June–November, 1926.

An Old Chester Secret. New York: Harper & Brothers, 1920. First published in *Harper's Weekly*, August–October, 1920.

Partners. New York: Harper & Brothers, 1913. First published as "A Fourth-Class Appointment" in *Harper's Monthly*, January, 1892.

Philip and His Wife. Boston: Houghton, Mifflin, 1894. First published in *Atlantic Monthly*, January–October, 1894.

The Promises of Alice. New York: Harper & Brothers, 1919. First published in *Ladies' Home Journal*, August–November, 1917.

The Rising Tide. New York: Harper & Brothers, 1916. First published in *Woman's Home Companion*, December, 1915–October, 1916.

Sidney. Boston: Houghton, Mifflin, 1890. First published in *Atlantic Monthly*, January–October, 1890.

The Story of a Child. Boston: Houghton, Mifflin, 1892. First published in *Atlantic Monthly,* September–November, 1892. Reissued as *The Story of a Child in Old Chester,* Boston: Houghton, Mifflin, 1906.

The Vehement Flame. New York: Harper & Brothers, 1922. First published in *Woman's Home Companion,* December, 1921–June, 1922.

The Voice. New York: Harper & Brothers, 1912. First published in *Harper's Monthly,* September, 1902.

The Way to Peace. New York: Harper & Brothers, 1910. First published in *Ladies' Home Journal,* March–April, 1909.

Where the Laborers Are Few. New York: Harper & Brothers, 1909. First published in *Harper's Monthly,* October, 1898.

2. Collected Essays and Short Fiction

Around Old Chester. New York: Harper & Brothers, 1915. Reprints "The Voice" and "An Encore." Short stories from *Harper's Monthly:* "Turn About," December, 1913–January, 1914; "The Harvest of Fear," June–July, 1914; "The Thief," July, 1898; "Miss Clara's Perseus," September–October, 1914. Also "The Third Volume" from *Delineator,* May–June, 1915.

The Common Way. New York: Harper & Brothers, 1904. Essays reprinted from *Harper's Bazar:* "On the Shelf" titled "The Shelf," April, 1902; "Aunts," April, 1903; "The Passing of Dora," August, 1902; "Love My Dog" titled "Twentieth Century Letters No. 1," February, 1903; "Acquaintance with Grief," October, 1903; "Concerning Glass Houses," July, 1904; "Concerning Christmas Giving," December, 1904; "To the Girl Who Writes" titled "The Girl Who Writes," July 14, 1900. Also "Concerning Church-Going" from *Independent,* October 15, 1903; "The Tyranny of Things."

Dr. Lavendar's People. New York: Harper & Brothers, 1903. Reprints. New York: AMS Press, 1969; New York: Garrett Press, 1969; Freeport, New York: Books for Libraries Press, 1970; St. Clair Shores, Mich.: Scholarly Press, 1970. Short stories from *Harper's Monthly:* "The Apotheosis of the Reverend Mr. Spangler," December, 1902; "The Note," September, 1903; "The Grasshopper and the Ant," October, 1903; "Amelia," August, 1903; "An Exceeding High Mountain," November, 1903; "At the Stuffed Animal House," May, 1903.

Mr. Tommy Dove and Other Stories. Boston: Houghton, Mifflin, 1893. Reprint: Freeport, N.Y.: Books for Libraries Press, 1969. Short stories "Mr. Tommy Dove" from *Atlantic Monthly,* January, 1889; "The Face on the Wall" from *Harper's Monthly,* March, 1893; "Elizabeth"; "At Whose Door?"; "A Fourth-Class Appointment" from *Harper's Monthly,* January, 1892.

New Friends in Old Chester. New York: Harper & Brothers, 1924. Reprints "An Old Chester Secret." Also novelettes: "The Eliots' Katy" from *Harper's Weekly*, December, 1923–February, 1924; "How *COULD* She!" titled "When Old Chester Wondered" in *Harper's Monthly*, August–October, 1921.

Old Chester Days. New York: Harper & Brothers, 1937. Reprint: Freeport, N.Y.: Books for Libraries, 1970. Reprints short stories from other collections: "The Note," "At the Stuffed Animal House," "The Grasshopper and the Ant," "Good for the Soul," "An Encore," "The Voice," "The Third Volume," "An Exceeding High Mountain."

Old Chester Tales. New York: Harper & Brothers, 1898. Reprints. New York: AMS Press, 1969; New York: Garrett Press, 1969; New York: Greenwood Press, 1969. Short stories reprinted from *Harper's Monthly:* "The Promises of Dorothea," April, 1898; "Good for the Soul," May, 1898; "Miss Maria," June, 1898; "The Child's Mother," August, 1898; "Justice and the Judge," September, 1898; "Where the Laborers Are Few," October, 1898; "Sally," November, 1898; "The Unexpectedness of Mr. Horace Shields," December, 1898.

R.J.'s Mother and Some Other Stories. New York: Harper & Brothers, 1908. Reprints. "R.J.'s Mother" from *Harper's Monthly*, August, 1907; "The Mormon" titled "An Exploiter of Souls" in *Harper's Monthly*, August, 1904; "Many Waters," *Collier's*, May 13, 1905; "House of Rimmon" titled "The Wisdom of Fools" in *Harper's Monthly*, April, 1897; "A Black Drop," *Collier's*, May 2–9, 1908; "The White Feather," *Century Magazine*, July, 1904.

Small Things. New York: D. Appleton & Co., 1919. Essays from *Woman's Home Companion:* "Facing France," May, 1918; "Dry-Eyed, Heartbroken, Laughing," June, 1918; "Their Great Moments," October, 1918; "Napoleon—and Others," July, 1918; "Things We Thought Were Big," August, 1918; "Marching Gayly," November, 1918; "The Fellowship of Tears" titled "Frightfulness," December, 1918; "The Regal Soul," January, 1919; "We Decide the Kaiser's Fate," April, 1919. Also "Beads—Paris—January, 1918" from *Harper's Monthly*, July, 1918; "We'll Stamp the Beast Out," *American Magazine*, December, 1918; "First That Which Is Natural" called "The American Girl 'Over There' " in *Ladies' Home Journal*, October, 1918.

The Wisdom of Fools. Boston: Houghton, Mifflin, 1897. Reprint: Freeport, N.Y.: Books for Libraries Press, 1969. Short stories: "Where Ignorance Is Bliss, 'Tis Folly To Be Wise"; "House of Rimmon" titled "The Wisdom of Fools" in *Harper's Monthly*, April, 1897; "Counting the Cost," *Pocket Magazine*, August, 1896; "The Law,

Or the Gospel" called "One Woman's Story: A Study" in *Cosmopolitan*, February, 1896.

3. Uncollected Essays and Short Fiction

Essays

"The Badness of Good People." *Ladies' Home Journal*, April, 1914.
"The Change in the Feminine Ideal." *Atlantic Monthly*, March, 1910.
"Christmas Giving." *Book Buyer*, December, 1889.
"Concerning Sinners." *Harper's Bazar*, July, 1905.
"Concerning the Saints." *Harper's Bazar*, June, 1905.
"A Deep-Seated Trouble." *Good Housekeeping*, February, 1905.
"The Doors of Silence: A Discussion of the Possibilities of Communication with Those Who Have Died." *Woman's Home Companion*, November, 1919.
"The Doors of Silence: Are They Closed Forever When Those We Love Have Died?" *Woman's Home Companion*, December, 1919.
"The Doors of Silence: If the Cap Fits." *Woman's Home Companion*, January, 1920.
"Dwarfs." *Harper's Bazar*, January, 1904.
"The Ethics of the Novel." *Independent*, April 13, 1899.
"Gardening and Life." *Harper's Bazar*, June 30, 1900.
"Giving–A Christmas Editorial." *Woman's Home Companion*, December, 1916.
"The Great Determination." *Woman's Home Companion*, November, 1923.
"I Didn't Know—." *Ladies' Home Journal*, March, 1907.
"In the Long Run What Difference Does the Rain Make?" *Ladies' Home Journal*, May, 1913.
"Individualism and Social Responsibility." *Independent*, May 23, 1901.
"Jonquils." *Good Housekeeping*, August, 1904.
"The Joys of Gardening." *Country Life in America*, March 1, 1911.
"The Light Which Is Darkness." *Harper's Monthly*, June, 1919.
"A Menace to Literature." *North American Review*, February, 1894.
"The New Woman Who Would Do Things." *Ladies' Home Journal*, September, 1907.
"The Novel with a Purpose." *Independent*, April 20, 1899.
"Old Unhappy Far-Off Things." *Woman's Home Companion*, April, 1934.
"Phillips Brooks." *Atlantic Monthly*, July, 1940.
"A Representative Publisher." *Outlook*, November 2, 1895.
"Save Christmas!" *Harper's Bazar*, December, 1912.
"A Sense of Opportunity." *Good Housekeeping*, October, 1910.

"Shall I Try to Write Stories?" *Woman's Home Companion,* March, 1919.
"Snakes in Ireland." *Harper's Bazar,* November, 1904.
"Snakes in Ireland: A Little Talk About the Compensations of Middle Age." *Woman's Home Companion,* May, 1917.
"Studies of Great Women." *Harper's Bazar:* "Cleopatra," October 27, 1900; "Madame Recamier," November 24, 1900; "Cornelia," December 22, 1900; "Elizabeth," January 19, 1901; "Madame de Maintenon," February 2, 1901; "Joan of Arc," February 23, 1901; "Angelica Kauffmann," April 20, 1901; "Charlotte Corday," July, 1901.)
"The Third Way in Woman Suffrage." *Ladies' Home Journal,* January, 1913.
"The Three S's." *Woman's Home Companion,* January, 1918.
"The Tight Rope of Pretense." *Ladies' Home Journal,* June, 1921.
"The Truth of the Novel." *Independent,* April 6, 1899.
"The Value of the Novel." *Independent,* March 30, 1899.
"We—The Unimportant People." *Ladies' Home Journal,* November, 1920.
"What Is A Novel?" *Bookman,* February, 1916.
"What, Really, Is Patriotism?" *Ladies' Home Journal,* July, 1916.
"When I Was Your Age." *Good Housekeeping,* December, 1913.
"The Wickedness of Growing Old." *Harper's Bazar,* February, 1905.
"Woman in the Market Place." *Independent,* May 22, 1916.

Fiction
"The Immediate Jewel." *Harper's Monthly,* December, 1903.
"The Waiting Hand." *Century Magazine,* July, 1909.

4. Autobiographies, Poetry, Miscellaneous
Confession. Hampton, Va.: Hampton Institute Press, 1933[?].
Florida Days. Boston: Little, Brown & Co., 1889.
Golden Yesterdays. New York: Harper & Brothers, 1941. First published in *Woman's Home Companion,* June–September, 1941.
If This Be I, As I Suppose It Be. New York: D. Appleton–Century, 1935.
The Old Garden and Other Verses. Boston: Houghton, Mifflin, & Co., 1886.
"A Peak in Darien" in *The Case For and Against Psychial Belief.* Worcester, Mass.: Clark University, 1927. Reprinted as "Though Inland Far We Be—." Hampton, Va.: Hampton Institute, 1932.
The Story of Delia. Boston: The House of Mercy, 1920[?].

SECONDARY SOURCES

1. Adaptations of Deland Works

Kemper, Sallie. *An Old Chester Secret.* Boston: Boston Theatre Guild Plays, 1924. One-act play.

Thompson, Charlotte. *The Awakening of Helena Richie.* New York: A. Kauser, ca. 1908. Four-act play.

Vosburgh, Maude B. *Miss Maria.* New York: Samuel French, 1917. One-act play.

2. Books and Parts of Books

Adelman, Joseph. *Famous Women.* New York: Ellis M. Lonow Co., 1926. Includes a capsule biography of Deland.

Dodd, Loring Holmes. *Celebrities at Our Hearthside.* Boston: Dresser, Chapman & Grimes, 1959. Portraits of speakers at Clark University's arts lectures. Deland is discussed in "The Friendliness of Margaret Deland."

Herron, Ima H. *The Small Town in American Literature.* Durham, N.C.: Duke University Press, 1939. Discusses Old Chester and Dr. Lavendar, calling Old Chester an extension of the New England village.

McNall, Sally Allen. *Who Is In The House? A Psychological Study of Two Centuries of Women's Fiction in America, 1795 to the Present.* New York: Elsevier, 1981. Calls the mothers in *The Iron Woman* and *The Promises of Alice* indifferent.

Overton, Grant. *The Women Who Make Our Novels.* rev. ed. New York: Dodd, Mead & Co., 1928. Discusses Deland's work generally, focusing on *The Iron Woman.*

Pattee, Fred Lewis. *A History of American Literature Since 1870.* New York: Century Co., 1917. Discusses *John Ward, Preacher* as revolt against a system of beliefs; says that Deland's novels deal with great ethical forces.

Quinn, Arthur Hobson. *American Fiction: An Historical and Critical Survey.* New York: D. Appleton–Century, 1936. Describes Deland as a realist and the Old Chester stories as the peak of her achievement.

Reep, Diana. *The Rescue and Romance: Popular Novels Before World War I.* Bowling Green, Ohio: Bowling Green Popular Press, 1982. *The Rising Tide* and the liberated heroine.

Smith, Herbert F. *The Popular American Novel 1865–1920.* Boston: Twayne, 1980. Good discussion of Deland as more "modern" than her contemporary, Gertrude Atherton. Surveys *John Ward, Preacher, The Awakening of Helena Richie,* and Old Chester stories.

Van Doren, Carl. *Contemporary American Novelists 1900–1920.* New York: Macmillan, 1931. Deland's Old Chester stories as local color. Comments that her novels are overly sentimental.

Welter, Barbara. *Dimity Convictions: The American Woman in the Nineteenth Century.* Athens, Ohio: Ohio University Press, 1976. Discusses *John Ward, Preacher* and Deland as a novelist of religious controversy.

Williams, Blanche. *Our Short Story Writers.* New York: Moffat, Yard & Co., 1920. Presents a full chapter on the Old Chester stories, stressing Deland's humor and treatment of women.

3. Articles

Alden, Henry Mills. "The Author of *The Iron Woman.*" *Outlook* 99 (November 11, 1911):628–32. Deland's work, particularly the creation of Old Chester and Mercer.

Chapple, Joe Mitchell. "Margaret Deland." *National Magazine* (Boston) 9 (1899):522–29. An interview with Deland, containing her comments on her writing background and public response.

Ford, Mary K. "Some Representative American Story Tellers. IV—Margaret Deland." *Bookman* 25 (1907):511–19. Ethical questions in Deland's novels discussed.

Gould, Marjorie D. "Of Margaret Deland and 'Old Chester.' " *Colby Library Quarterly* 2(1944):167–70. Briefly reviews Deland's Old Chester stories with mention of her personal background.

Howe, M. A. De Wolfe. "*Margaret Deland: A Study in Influences.*" *Outlook* 84 (November 24, 1906):730–34. Praises the Old Chester stories and Deland's skill at portraying children. Includes some biographical information.

Humphry, James, III. "The Works of Margaret Deland." *Colby Library Quarterly* 2 (1944):134–40. Reviews Deland's life and work because the Colby College library received a collection of most of her works.

Kantor, J. R. K. "*The Damnation of Theron Ware* and *John Ward, Preacher.*" *Serif* 3 (1966):16–21. Asserts that Harold Frederic knew Deland's novel and used some of her themes in his book.

McDonald, Donald. "Mrs. Deland's Childhood." *Outlook* 64 (February 17, 1900):407–10. Written by a friend of Deland's, the article discusses her childhood and the influences that appeared in her fiction.

McIlvaine, Robert. "Two Awakenings: Edna Pontellier and Helena Richie." *Regionalism and the Female Imagination* 4 (1979):44–48. Speculates that Deland knew of Kate Chopin's *The Awakening* and wrote a response in *The Awakening of Helena Richie.*

Macmillan, D. "Recent Religious Novels and the Moral Theory of Another Life." *Scots Magazine* 6 (1890):321–35. Discusses the recent appearance of novels dealing seriously with religious issues; focuses on *John Ward, Preacher* and *The Story of an African Farm* by Olive Schreiner.

O'Connor, T. P. "T. P. O'Connor Discovers Margaret Deland." *Harper's Weekly,* June 16, 1906, pp. 859, 861. Reality in Old Chester stories.

Purdy, Lucia. "Mrs. Deland at Home." *Critic* 33 (1898):33–39. Describes Deland's personality, home life, and work habits.

Wilson, Albert Frederick. "Can Children Be Taught to Write?" *Good Housekeeping* 61 (1915):44–50. Includes Deland with other women writers and quotes her on what she read as a child and her early ambitions in writing.

Index